# EXTREME DIVIN

Andrea Ballerini · Luciana Rota

◆

# EXTREME DIVING

## HISTORY, TECHNIQUES, RUNS

**UNIVERSE PUBLISHING**

# Contents

# Origins and myth

Man's relationship with the sea is ancient, and fraught with tragedy and triumph. The historical documents and folk legends of all civilizations bordering great waters contain references to humans who have descended into the depths of the sea. Not surprisingly, Greek mythology speaks of a goddess, Aphrodite, born out of the sea and married to Hephaistos, the earth god who fell from Olympus into an underwater cave.

Mythology and legend aside, the first official European record of what would today be considered a "free dive" dates from 1913. An Italian ship, the *Regina Margherita*, was anchored in a Grecian port, about to set sail, when one of its anchors became entangled in the seabed. A Greek fisherman, Gheorghios Statti, dived to a depth of 253 feet to retrieve the anchor. With no mask, fins, or regulator, he plunged to a depth not reached until many years later by "professional" free divers.

Even though webbed flippers are to be found among Leonardo da Vinci's studies regarding the sea, the genuine article appeared on the scene in 1935, when a Frenchman, De Corelieu, sold feet flippers for underwater swimmers. The modern concept of diving goggles also emerged in France in the 1930s, although a chronicle of 1300 tells of pearl hunters in the Persian Gulf wearing ace masks made from turtle shells, polished until perfectly transparent.

A diver exploring a cave is privy to the intense spectacle of the underwater world. The angelfish in this photo are a brightly colored tropical species that favor shoals and coral reefs.

# Underwater archaeology

The sea jealously guards the traces of our past. Much of the evidence of ancient civilizations is the exclusive property of the murky depths. The fascination experienced when diving in search of history is an indescribable sensation. Discovering an underwater city, its mansions and temples; coming across an ancient ship and brushing past its keel to examine its cargo; the myth of Atlantis and the dream of being the first to reach it has driven men and women to defy the depths of the sea. A scuba diver conducting archaeological research must be well versed in all diving, search, and retrieval equipment. When rereading history in the sea's great natural archives we must also respect the laws and regulations; every find, from an amphora to a small lantern handle must eventually be turned over to the proper authorities. Not every treasure hunter complies with these rules, and areas rich in historic relics have been plundered and continue to be plundered for the profit of sales to private collectors. Countless discoveries made by divers in seas and lakes all over the world have helped us to evaluate history and enrich our knowledge, making this one of the most enthralling underwater activities. For this reason, the various courses available include some which specialize in marine archaeology. Under the guidance of trained instructors you can set off to search and explore known areas or venture farther afield in the world's largest museum: the sea.

Top Left: here lie the remains of a Japanese cargo ship that sank in the Strait of Bonifacio in bad weather around 1968. Beaten against the rocks by a southwesterly gale, the ship sank and has over the years become a popular destination for archaeology enthusiasts.

Center: a diver exploring the wreck of what was formerly a manned landing craft. Discovered at a depth of approximately 98 feet north of the island of Ponza in Italy, it dates from the Second World War.

Bottom Left: exploring a wreck. This anti-aircraft gun sank with the rest of the craft.

# Exploring the sea

To dive is above all a formidable adventure, an exploration of another universe full of unimaginable wonders. The sea offers such a wide range of "encounters" that every dive becomes a journey in itself. In order to best assimilate this environment, we must first respect it and therefore not upset the delicate balance that governs there. Such is the animation of the sea that you can find hundreds of living forms and as many vegetable species in just a few square feet. Each sea has different characteristics, including temperature, color, transparency, taste, and even sound: that of waves breaking on coral reefs as you dive is different from that of the sea "whiplashing" hard cliff faces. Exploring the sea is different for each diver depending on the goals involved: biologists seek life and the secrets of marine organisms; photographers seek to capture a fleeting moment of beauty with their cameras; pearl and coral divers test personal limits; archaeologists study the past in the natural archives that have been built up by the sea beds over the centuries.

Opposite page: shapes and colors change according to the light and temperature underwater. The plays of light and transparencies created by some fish are impossible to describe and must be seen in situ: a diver has reached a cavity and discovered a species of alcyonaria. Nearly a thousand species of building corals exist in the most varied shapes.

Corals and gorgonians can often be found at shallow depths, sometimes less than 33 feet in poorly lit zones, such as caves.

Red gorgonians often become a sort of nursery for certain fish species. Here they are "inhabited" by a spotted dogfish, a shark typically found in the Mediterranean that has laid its eggs here to grow safely.

A simple strategy suffices for approaching fish in close proximity in the Mediterranean. The divers open a sea urchin and the hungry rockfish dash in.

A close-up of a scorpion fish, a common inhabitant of tropical seas.

A tropical madrepore.

Above Left: a fin of a typical tropical fish, which has directional and stabilizing functions. Above Center: a parrot fish; note the powerful teeth. Above Right: a detail of the eye. This is a non-migratory fish that feeds on the polyps contained in the madrepores. Below Left: tropical corvinus do not pass unnoticed with their distinctive black and white stripes alternated with bright golden yellow. This is another non-migratory species that lives in coral reefs. Below Right: a large starfish, which are often found on the Mediterranean seabed.

# Marine biology

The sea is really in both physical and chemical terms a biologically varied and complex world. The possibility of diving with regulators has enabled scientific and biological researchers to observe the countless animal and vegetable species of the seas in their own habitat. Before scuba diving, studies were conducted inside laboratories on subjects "forced" to live in unnatural environments. Scientifically speaking, the marine environment is divided into two zones: the neritic or littoral zone, between 0 and 656 feet in depth, and the pelagic zone, which comprises the deep waters off the coasts. For a biologist diver, usually, the first research zone is "littoral" (down to a depth of 115 feet), where photophilic algae (lovers of light), sea urchins, gastropod and lamellibranch mollusks, and posidonias can be found. In this first zone the light is natural but as you dive deeper other organisms are encountered including corals. The chance to follow organized courses in marine biology encourages many divers to improve their knowledge so as to approach the marine world with better training and awareness. Often the sea is treated like a large rubbish bin, upseting the equilibrium of the ecosystem. Thus, various habitats undergo changes that affect the development of all species. Marine biology permits the control of and research into these phenomena, and allows professional management of natural oases and marine parks.

Many dozens of varieties of starfish inhabit the ocean. From top to botton: a tropical starfish; *Echinaster sepositus*; *Alcyonium palmatum* called "St. Peter's Hand"; *Corallo rubrum*.

Underwater encounters: here a diver makes the acquaintance of a tropical-water turtle. The large sea turtle is a sociable sort, quite tolerant of humans.

# The seabed

While the surface of the sea appears to us as rather planar, the sea bottom is a wholly different scape. Like mountain ranges on land, the bottom of the North Atlantic Ocean is made up of a chain of ridges and fissures, which emerge above the water to form the Azores and Iceland at either end. The South Atlantic Ocean consists of muddy plains and valleys that resemble canyons. The Pacific is the most extensive geo-graphic unit on our planet and its waters contain the highest peaks (Haway 31,495 feet) and deepest trenches (Mariana trench 35,760 feet).

Aside from the benefits of marine biology, exploring the seabed allows analysis of major geological and seismic phenomena. This type of diving and exploration requires the highest degree of training plus sophisticated instruments and equipment.

# Record table

**ABSOLUTE VARIABLE BALLAST DIVING**

| YEAR | LOCATION | DIVER | NATIONALITY | DEPTH (feet) |
|---|---|---|---|---|
| 1949 | Naples | Raimondo Bucher | Italy | -98 |
| 1951 | Naples | Ennio Falco | Italy | -115 |
| 1951 | Naples | Alberto Novelli | Italy | -115 |
| 1952 | Capri | Raimondo Bucher | Italy | -128 |
| 1956 | Rapallo | Ennio Falco | Italy | -135 |
| 1956 | Rapallo | Alberto Novelli | Italy | -135 |
| 1960 | Rio de Janeiro | Americo Santarelli | Brazil | -141 |
| 1960 | Circeo | Americo Santarelli | Brazil | -144 |
| 1960 | Siracusa | Enzo Maiorca | Italy | -148 |
| 1960 | S. Margherita Ligure | Americo Santarelli | Brazil | -151 |
| 1960 | Siracusa | Enzo Maiorca | Italy | -161 |
| 1961 | Siracusa | Enzo Maiorca | Italy | -164 |
| 1962 | Ustica | Enzo Maiorca | Italy | -167 |
| 1964 | Siracusa | Enzo Maiorca | Italy | -174 |
| 1965 | Acireale | Enzo Maiorca | Italy | -177 |
| 1965 | Polynesia | Teteke Williams | Polynesia | -194 |
| 1966 | Bahamas | Jacques Mayol | France | -197 |
| 1966 | Siracusa | Enzo Maiorca | Italy | -203 |
| 1967 | Florida | Bob Croft | USA | -210 |
| 1967 | Cuba | Enzo Maiorca | Italy | -210 |
| 1967 | Florida | Bob Croft | USA | -230 |
| 1967 | Florida | Jacques Mayol | France | -233 |
| 1968 | Florida | Bob Croft | USA | -239 |
| 1970 | Ognina | Enzo Maiorca | Italy | -243 |
| 1970 | Futo | Jacques Mayol | France | -246 |
| 1970 | Futo | Jacques Mayol | France | -249 |
| 1971 | Siracusa | Enzo Maiorca | Italy | -253 |
| 1972 | Ognina | Enzo Maiorca | Italy | -256 |
| 1973 | Genoa | Enzo Maiorca | Italy | -262 |
| 1973 | Isola d'Elba | Jacques Mayol | France | -282 |
| 1974 | Sorrento | Enzo Maiorca | Italy | -285 |
| 1975 | Island of Elba | Jacques Mayol | France | -302 |
| 1976 | Island of Elba | Jacques Mayol | France | -331 |
| 1983 | Island of Elba | Jacques Mayol | France | -344 |
| 1989 | Island of Elba | Angela Bandini | Italy | -351 |
| 1989 | Cuba | Pipin Ferreras | Cuba | -367 |
| 1991 | Siracusa | Pipin Ferreras | Cuba | -377 |
| 1991 | Island of Elba | Umberto Pelizzari | Italy | -387 |
| 1992 | Ustica | Pipin Ferreras | Cuba | -393 |
| 1993 | Montecristo | Umberto Pelizzari | Italy | -404 |
| 1993 | Bahamas | Pipin Ferreras | Cuba | -410 |
| 1994 | Siracusa | Pipin Ferreras | Cuba | -413 |
| 1994 | Florida | Pipin Ferreras | Cuba | -417 |
| 1995 | Siracusa | Pipin Ferreras | Cuba | -420 |
| 1996 | Villasimius | Umberto Pelizzari | Italy | -430 |
| 1998 | Sardinia | Gianluca Genoni | Italy | -443 |
| 1999 | Nice | Loïc Leferme | France | -449 |
| 1999 | Liguria | Umberto Pelizzari | Italy | -492 |

(table updated to november 1999)

*continue on p. 34*

# First divers

Before explaining the various levels and specialized branches that have gradually emerged in diving, we must first discuss your initial dives, and the essential training involved. The first dives serve to steer the diver toward a subsequent specialization or simply toward courses that provide better knowledge of the sea in accordance with personal interests, from biology to photography. Anyone following the guidelines and rules of modern scuba diving can enter this world—all that is required is a pair of fins, a mask, and a desire to explore the underwater environment with the same respect asked of the terrestrial one. The first fundamental rule of underwater activity is to always dive in pairs; this is not meant to be restrictive, but an opportunity to share the myriad experiences offered by the underwater world with one or more travel companions. It is also easier to prepare for dives in pairs, helping each other to kit up and enter the water, not to mention coping with emergencies. The next fundamental step is to familiarize yourself with the necessary equipment.

The first dives do not require a great deal of equipment but it is important for a novice to learn its characteristics, correct use, and maintenance. During the first group outings take advantage of the opportunity to compare your first experiences with others, thus fostering your ability to dive safely and pleasurably. Fins, masks, regulator, weight belt, wetsuit, the indispensable knife, and a marker buoy are the first "tools" that a novice must learn to use.

# Preparation

A proper approach to underwater activities includes some fitness training, which will lay the foundation for subsequent specialization. Although underwater diving requires no special talents or significant physical requisites, you will achieve the best results by training within the specific water environment. The very first stage in this training is both physical and mental, aimed in particular at acquiring the notion of "aqua-ability." No specific exercises are required initially, but it is crucial that you feel at home in the water, and it doesn't hurt to improve your breaststroke or crawl. This will enable you to perform dives in an optimum state: personal confidence is a major contribution to effortless and efficient movements in the water. The next step, after surface swimming, consists of specific simple exercises that focus on coordinating movement with breathing.

**SUBMERGING**
A novice diver is ready to perform a basic movement: submerging. He is about to do a tucked roll to reach the bottom.

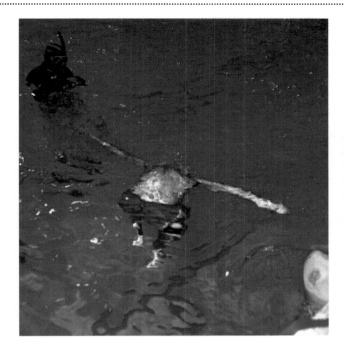

**TUCKED ROLL**
Above: after learning the correct diving position, you proceed to the unequipped "tucked roll." This exercise should be repeated until it becomes second nature, a fluid movement that requires no excess energy.

**IN THE WATER**
Below: as well as unequipped physical training, it is also important in the initial stages to develop a certain familiarity with your essential equipment. These water outings made with fins and mask are highly recommended. This is the first time you try breathing with scuba equipment.

**IMPROVING STAMINA**
Below: free-standing exercise: the diver performs the backstroke, using just the arms. This basic exercise helps improve stamina in the water and strengthen the arms, the body's principal propeller.

**IN PAIRS**
Above: after the initial training on your own, the group or pair work begins. Learning to coordinate your movements with other divers will help you gain the necessary fluidity in the water and increase your operating capacity when free-diving. This will also accustom you to normal diving situations that must, for safety reasons, always involve at least two divers.

# Training

Once you have made your preparations and feel at ease in the water, you will find that training exercises become more specific. Even though some of these exercises may appear simple at first, it's important that you learn to execute them properly so that when put to the test on later dives you will automatically know how to best exploit the hydrodynamic thrust of movements as well as avoid pointless and tiring movements that only hamper your progress in the water. With this series of set exercises, you will gradually acquire important mental and physical control that will allow you to be more relaxed when performing basic movements underwater.

**EXECUTING A TUCKED ROLL TO DIVE**
In this apparently simple exercise it is vital to learn how to bring your arms and legs close to your chest in order to create the smallest possible surface area in the water and turn easily and fluidly. To complete the movement, stretch your legs and push off strong enough to take you to the bottom, employing a modified breaststroke with the arms if necessary.

## KICKING IN THE WATER

Below: this position shows the benefit in hydrodynamic thrust obtained when you stretch your legs. Fully stretched legs optimize the thrust, downward in this case.

### FIRST ARM-STROKES OR STARTING POSITION

(1) After reaching the bottom in the fully stretched starting position, begin swimming in what is called "underwater breaststroke".

(2, 3) In this case, the arm and leg movements are a little different than those of a "surface breaststroke," to exploit a greater hydrodynamic thrust.

(4) Lastly, the leg-stroke, giving the body a decisive push forward in the water.

### GONE BACK FROM THE BOTTON WITH LEGS TO SQUARE

These photos illustrate a position you can use to rest underwater, or as the initial phase of resurfacing slowly. It is important to learn different positions of equilibrium underwater—a varied repertoire will serve you well on more complicated dives.

### FLIP-OVER

The rest position is the beginning of executing the flip-over. With toes pointing toward the surface and head straight, arms and legs should be parallel.

### INVERTED FLIP-OVER

The body's position for this movement is exactly the same as the previous one, just inverted 180 degrees.

## CLEARING YOUR MASK
This is typically the first of the equipped exercises, but only involves a face mask. Begin by resting your knees on the bottom of the pool, and tilt your head back, looking up toward the surface. Pull your mask away from your face from the bottom of the mask.

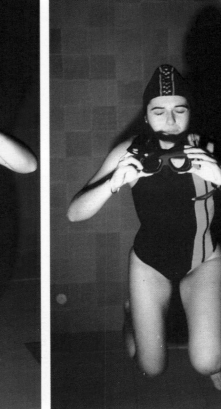

## RETRIEVING AND CLEARING YOUR MASK
Learning to retrieve and put on your mask underwater is also an essential exercise, which will come in handy should you temporarily lose your mask underwater. Simulate the act of "dropping" the mask, retreive it, and put it back on, clearing it as described above.

# Licenses

The Professional Association of Diving Instructors (PADI), which is the largest diving organization in America, has operated for thirty-four years throughout the country with organized scuba diving training structures.

The PADI is recognized all over the world and through its national technical center, federal schools, outlying technical centers, associated clubs, and approved sea points, it organizes training courses for federal licenses in the various specialist branches. These licenses are recognized by the R.S.T.C. (Recreational Scuba Training Council) in Europe and the Japanese bodies. The R.S.T.C. is today considered the world's leading body, with international standards and rules that aim to regulate and standardize underwater activities practiced in all countries. The licenses issued by PADI are: Basic Diving, Open Water Diving, Advanced Open Water Diving, Trainee Instructor, Instructor, and Master Instructor.

Specialization may be achieved through various courses and these are: night dive, boat dive, dry suit dive, underwater naturalist dive, wreck dive, altitude dive, multilevel dive, search and recovery dive, underwater photography dive, underwater videography dive and diver propulsion vehicle drive.

## LICENSES

### Basic Diving
This qualifies a diver for open water diving to maximum depths of 66 feet with a partner holding at least the same license.

### Open-Water Diving
This qualifies a diver for open-water diving to maximum depths of 98 feet that do not require decompression.

### Advanced Open-Water Diving
This qualifies a diver for dives to maximum depths of 131 feet that do not require decompression.

### Trainee Instructor
This qualifies a diver to assist an instructor with courses.

### Instructor
This qualifies a person to teach theory and practice at all levels in enclosed and open water.

### Master Instructor
This qualifies a person to teach theory and practice at all levels in enclosed and open water, to train and assess instructors, and to act as a federal commissioner.

## PADI THE LARGEST DIVER-TRAINING GROUP IN THE WORLD

PADI has many objectives, including.

1. To set minimum safety standards for the training of divers and instructors at various levels

2. To act as a qualified partner to governmental offices concerned with scuba safety standards thus ensuring consistent and effective regulations and laws

3. To create European and worldwide standards for diver and instructor training and enable an instructor to work anywhere in the world and a diver to dive safely with an internationally recognized license

4. To improve the public image of diving and of divers in general

# The courses

Initially, all you really need is a good mask and a pair of fins, starting off perhaps with a snorkeling course. The next step would be to discover where your particular interests lie, pursuing a course in photography, marine biology (the most popular), archaeology, wreck diving, or night diving. Tests for each course set at increasing degrees of difficulty qualify the trainee for higher levels as well as providing specific preparation for the chosen subject.

FIRST OUTING – BASIC COURSE

AN ADVANCED OPEN-WATER DIVE

ADVANCED OPEN-WATER DIVING COURSE

ADVANCED OPEN-WATER DIVING TRAINEE INSTRUCTOR COURSE

From top to bottom right:
1. A YOUNG DIVER
2. WRECK DIVING
3. NIGHT DIVING
4. SEARCH AND RESCUE
5. PHOTOGRAPHY COURSE

From top to bottom left:
1. DEEP DIVING TRAINEE INSTRUCTOR
2. CORAL REEF EXPLORATION, INSTRUCTOR EXAM COURSE
3-4. NITROX AND MARINE BIOLOGY

# Snorkeling

Scuba diving involves many complicated factors, and is traditionally introduced to the novice in a controlled environment such as a swimming pool. In this way, customary winter courses carried out in indoor swimming pools prepare new divers for their first spring or summer outings. Another practical introduction to diving is snorkeling.

Snorkeling was born as a fashionable leisure activity, particularly popular at seaside holiday resorts, but has, quite rightly, become a "specialization" and is taught in courses organized all over the world. It is quite simply an easy and safe way for everyone to try aquatic life before deciding whether to continue with underwater exploration and obtain various degrees of qualification.

No special swimming skills are required, but it is often on a snorkeling course that a swimmer decides to improve his or her style. As far as age is concerned, you must be at least fourteen years old before you can start to explore the attractions of the seabed and colors that are rarely seen on the surface.

Snorkeling can be practiced by anyone because the equipment used is light—just fins, a mask, and a snorkel tube for breathing. Generally, especially in tropical seas, a wetsuit is not necessary, just a T-shirt to protect against the powerful rays of the sun. Snorkeling allows you to explore the sea and its splendid coral reefs just below the surface, letting your body float, training your eyes to spot the marine life present in the first few feet of water.

Fins, mask, and a snorkel—and you are ready to set off and explore the sea.

It is advisable to start in groups with a qualified escort.

# Record table

*continued from p.18*

## CONSTANT BALLAST

| YEAR | LOCATION | ATHLETE | NATION | DEPTH (Feet) |
|---|---|---|---|---|
| 1978 | Island of Giglio | Stefano Makula | Italy | -164 |
| 1978 | Siracusa | Mario Imbesi | Italy | -171 |
| 1978 | Siracusa | Nuccio Imbesi | Italy | -171 |
| 1978 | Siracusa | Enzo Maiorca | Italy | -180 |
| 1979 | Siracusa | Enzo Liistro | Italy | -184 |
| 1980 | Siracusa | Nuccio Imbesi | Italy | -187 |
| 1981 | Ponza | Stefano Makula | Italy | -190 |
| 1981 | Island of Elba | Jacques Mayol | France | -200 |
| 1989 | Réunion | Frank Messegué | France | -203 |
| 1990 | Milazzo | Pipin Ferreras | Cuba | -206 |
| 1990 | Island of Elba | Umberto Pelizzari | Italy | -213 |
| 1991 | Island of Elba | Umberto Pelizzari | Italy | -220 |
| 1992 | Varadero | Pipin Ferreras | Cuba | -223 |
| 1992 | Ustica | Umberto Pelizzari | Italy | -230 |
| 1995 | Villasimius | Umberto Pelizzari | Italy | -236 |
| 1996 | Corsica | Michel Oliva | France | -236 |
| 1997 | Siracusa | Alejandro Ravelo | Cuba | -239 |
| 1997 | Porto Venere | Umberto Pelizzari | Italy | -246 |
| 1998 | Siracusa | Alejandro Ravelo | Cuba | -249 |
| 1998 | Liguria | Umberto Pelizzari | Italy | -262 |

## VARIABLE BALLAST

| YEAR | LOCATION | ATHLETE | NATION | DEPTH (Feet) |
|---|---|---|---|---|
| 1974 | Sorrento | Enzo Maiorca | Italy | -285 |
| 1991 | Milazzo | Pipin Ferreras | Cuba | -302 |
| 1991 | Island of Elba | Umberto Pelizzari | Italy | -312 |
| 1993 | Siracusa | Pipin Ferreras | Cuba | -315 |
| 1994 | Cala Gonone | Umberto Pelizzari | Italy | -331 |
| 1995 | Villasimius | Umberto Pelizzari | Italy | -344 |
| 1996 | Siracusa | Gianluca Genoni | Italy | -348 |
| 1996 | Villasimius | Umberto Pelizzari | Italy | -361 |
| 1997 | Siracusa | Alejandro Ravelo | Cuba | -364 |
| 1997 | Porto Venere | Umberto Pelizzari | Italy | -377 |
| 1997 | Sardinia | Gianluca Genoni | Italy | -394 |
| 1998 | Sardinia | Gianluca Genoni | Italy | -397 |

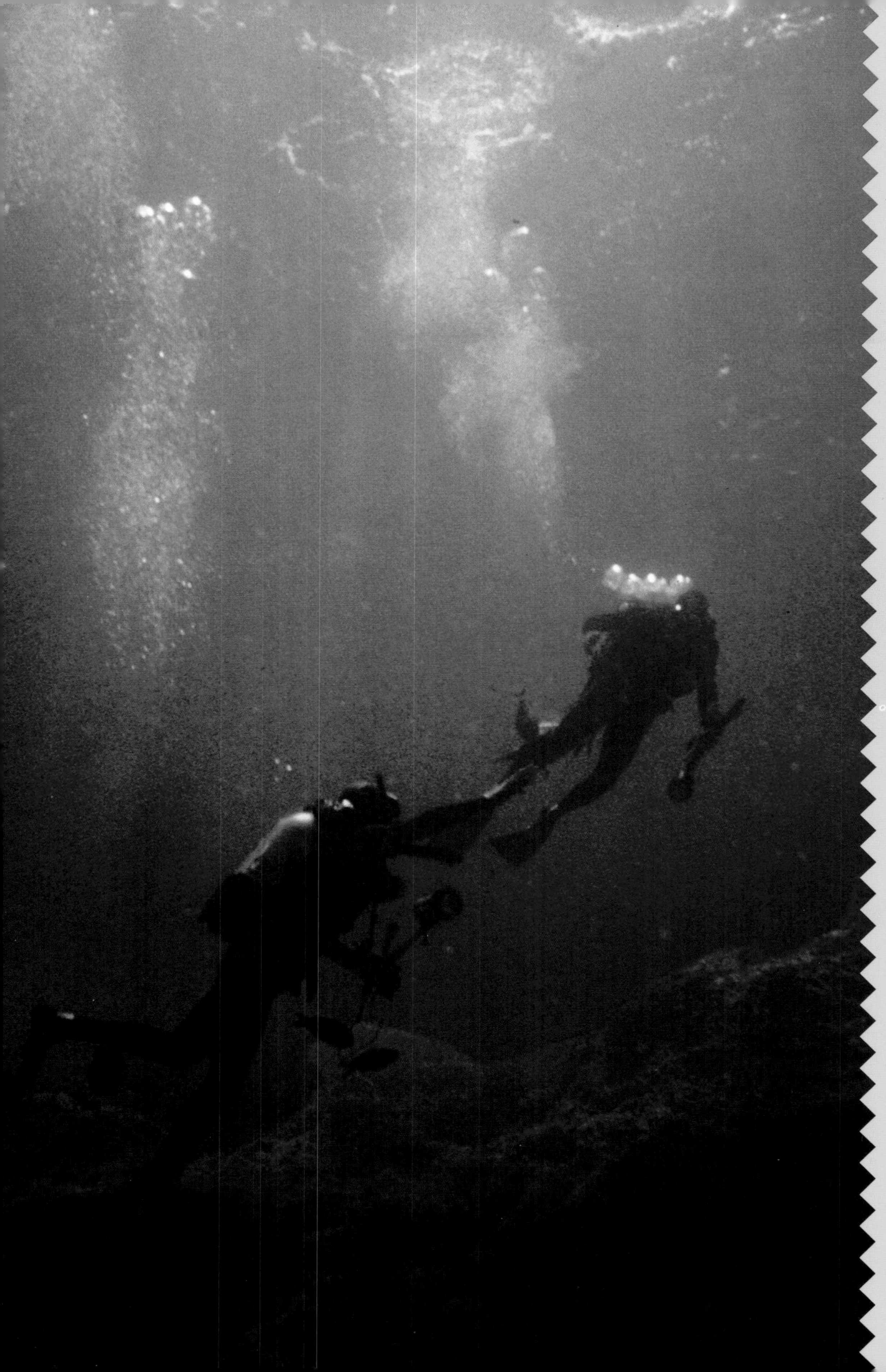

# SCUBA ACTIVITIES

# Recovery

Diving is never dangerous as long as you are familiar with your equipment and aware of the limits of your abilities. Although accidents often involve external factors, they are most commonly caused by superficial dive preparation and planning. Underwater assistance and "recovery" is a specific course that provides both technical training and teaches you how to cope with a dangerous situation. To handle a recovery correctly it is essential to have excellent knowledge of your own and the victim's equipment, as this may be crucial in accelerating recovery, transport, and resuscitation procedures. Statistical studies have highlighted a number of concurrent factors in diving accidents and the largest percentage regard inadequate training and careless dive preparation and planning; in the majority of cases this leads to insufficient decompression and errors in the calculation of subsequent dives.

Place the victim in a position that allows for the most ease of breathing.

The proper position allows movements to be executed more practically and faster.

**FIRST AID**
If a person is unconscious keep his face out of the water. It is best to hold the victim under the armpits, and crucial that you are able to keep the head out of the water and to remove equipment.

## HOLDING THE VICTIM BENEATH THE ARMPITS

This hold allows the rescuer to keep an arm free. The rescuer passes an arm beneath the victim's armpit from behind; using his other arm to press the victim's chest against him until the victim's head is resting on his shoulder on the same side. If the victim struggles, the rescuer can hold his arms still and block his head by pressing it against his shoulder.

The three photographs illustrate the hold on a struggling victim.

If the victim has a buoyancy compensator (BC) this can be inflated taking great care not to increase the volume of the jacket excessively and compress the chest, thus limiting breathing ability. Sometimes it is sufficient to eliminate the weight belt to facilitate floating if the victim is a swimmer or diver without scuba equipment.

If you are close to shore, do not waste time removing scuba equipment but go directly to the shore and start first aid without delay.

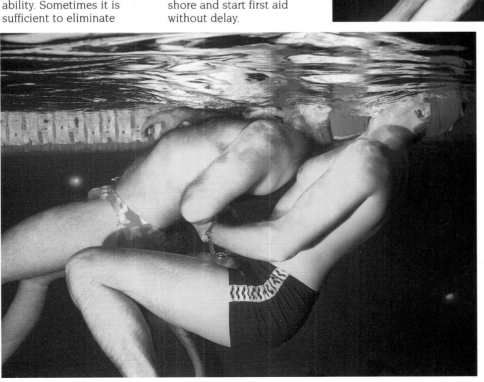

Avoiding the slightest risk of a diving accident requires knowledge, expertise, and caution. These must be combined with physical fitness, scrupulous dive planning, and complete, efficient equipment. Last but not least is the safety rule of always diving with a companion.

**SCUBA DIVER RECOVERY**
Once you have acquired the fundamental techniques of rescue, it is necessary to learn the different modes of transporting a fully equipped victim. These rescue maneuvers should be practiced till they become nearly automatic—so that in a real emergency you will not hesitate or panic.

**TRANSPORTING A TIRED DIVER**
In this case your co-diver is still conscious but requires assistance to reach the boat or shore. He may be suffering from cramps or breathing difficulties; he is not inactive but does need immediate help.

It is important to prepare yourself equally well for this type of rescue, because conscious victims are sometimes more difficult to transport as their disorganized movements may hamper your efforts.

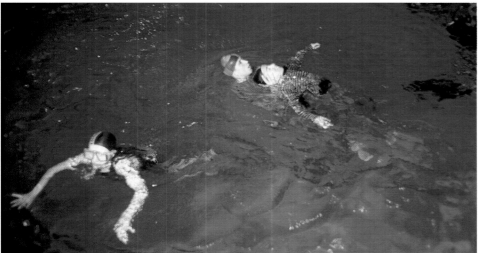

## RECOVERING A LARGER VICTIM

This technique is the same as the preceding one, but in this case it is important for the rescuer to learn what his or her exact limitations are, in order to avoid becoming a liability to the rescue effort.

## RECOVERY OF A FULLY DRESSED PERSON

Here the rescuer and the victim are both floating on their backs. The rescuing diver advances with the sole aid of a breaststroke leg motion.

Once the victim is secured it is necessary to remove him or her from the water. Opposite, the rescuer places the victim's hands on the edge of the "boat," and, while resting there without ever losing contact, pushes himself up to climb aboard first. From this superior vantage point, the rescuer may pull the victim aboard.

# Equipment

Scuba diving is a sport that requires a lot of complex and diverse equipment. Technically, the experience of diving begins once one puts one's head under the water, opens one's eyes, and observes underwater life. One can augment that very first experience with the use of very minimal equipment.

The first essential aids for underwater swimming are fins, mask, and a snorkel breathing tube. With these you are ready to dive and practice the activity better known as snorkeling, which is carried out in tropical seabeds or coral reefs or in a less exotic neighborhood lake. Fins permit more effortless swimming. Free-diving fins are long and narrow and the "blade" is often in nylon fiber. The face mask may be single or two-window and optical lenses can also be applied. The snorkel allows you to breathe with your face underwater. The next two pieces of fundamental underwater diving equipment are the weight belt, containing a number of lead weights; and the wetsuit, which consists of garments that will protect you against the cold or abrasions, and are constructed in Neoprene, an insulating material. Last, but no less crucial, are what could be called two safety tools. The first is a knife, to be considered principally as a means of defense and for practical use. The second is a "marker buoy," which consists of a floating ball with a flag. A marker buoy is required by law and the diver must swim under it within a range of 164 feet from its vertical pointer.

Besides a gauge, watch, and decompression tables, the compass is an essential instrument if you are to follow a set route and return to the starting point on a seabed with perhaps few landmarks. It is a must in cloudy water and on night dives.

When moving underwater, whether 3 or 66 feet beneath the surface, you must use the necessary instruments. The natural next step after the initial diving experience with mask and snorkel is to use a scuba (self-contained underwater breathing apparatus), which can be summed up as a buoyancy compensator, air tank, and regulator that enables you to breathe the compressed air contained in the tank.

The last instrument, and by far the most essential, is awareness, that is, knowledge of your personal ability to act in an environment that is not natural to humans. Improvisation or needless risk can endanger both you and others. By following a course under the guidance of expert instructors, you will learn to dive confidently and safely.

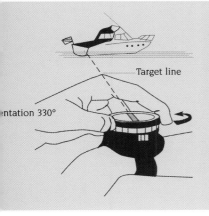

Target line

ntation 330°

A compass has a fixed circular section divided into 360 equal parts (degrees) and a mobile pointer positioned in the body concentric to it; thanks to the earth's magnetism it changes position to indicate north.

# Search and recovery

The accepted meaning of "search and recovery" covers several types of actions, ranging from exploration to emergencies.

The image of divers scouring the seabed in search of someone who has drowned or disappeared is perhaps the most common one, but often these professionals are also called upon to explore and search for wrecks or objects in difficult waters and currents. In activities such as these, the numerous search methods vary according to the zone, environmental conditions, and sometimes even the habits of those who perform them.

These methods include "circular searching," in which a dead weight is bound to a line secured to a surface buoy, and a second line, of varying length, is fixed to the weight. The diver, equipped with a compass, starts the search traveling in circles and extending the range of action as far as the line allows. Another type of method is the "pendulum search," in which the diver is tied to a point on land or on a boat. This system is used close to the coast and within fairly limited ranges. The "towed search" method is used for very large areas, usually operated by a boat on the surface. In the "jackstay search," a square area is marked off both on the surface and on the seabed using buoys and weights at the four corners so that the selected area can be systematically searched inch by inch.

## Knots

### FASTENING KNOTS

Although the use of snap hooks is becoming increasingly common, it is a good idea to learn some basic knots needed to secure an object of any kind using a line or a rope. Of the hundreds of knots known in the nautical world, a dozen or so will suffice to resolve the problem of connecting two objects in various situations. Right: starting from the top, a reef knot, single and double fisherman's bend a sheet bend.

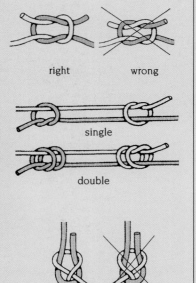

right wrong

single

double

right wrong

### HITCHES

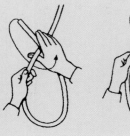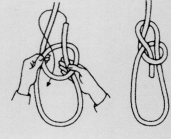

**BOWLINE KNOT**
This is the most classic knot and is especially reliable in an emergency. The drawing above shows how to tie it; the end (turned to tie the knot) must come out in the middle of the loop.

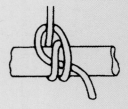

**ANCHOR KNOT**
Used to secure a rope to the anchor, this is also ideal for hanging a bucket or mooring to a ring.

Searching often leads to finding—in which case the process of recovery may commence, using various methods depending on the size of the object: cables only, harnesses, or lifting balloons. All search and recovery operations require a lot of coordination between the divers and the boat on the surface.

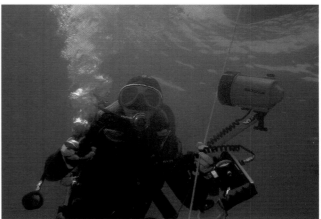

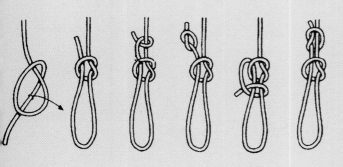

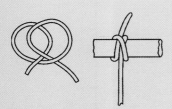

### CLOVE-HITCH KNOT
Quick and easy to tie and untie, this is perfect for hanging a load to a stay or a ring. It is also good for mooring.

### SAFETY LOOPS
A simple knot with its end closed is then finished off with various safety knots to prevent sliding. This is a very secure knot, not so easy to untie as the more traditional bowline knot.

### MISCELLANEOUS

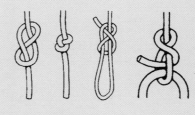

### FIGURE-EIGHT KNOT
This is normally used at the end of a rope, as a stop knot, or for making slip knots.

### BUTTERFLY KNOT
This creates a fixed fastening point with a grommet.

### SHEEPSHANK KNOT
This shortens a rope temporarily and holds well if taut, otherwise it loosens itself (above). The two loops can, if desired, be fixed with a thin line (below).

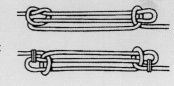

# Wreck diving

Archaeological diving has always stimulated great interest aroused by a curiosity for history and the environment, combined with a desire to explore the seabed and ponder its origins. In the diving world, research and archaeology have also followed a course that has led to the creation of international regulations based on respect for the environment, the history of the earth's surface, and marine life. Continuing specialization in the archaeological scuba diving sector has also produced a specific diving technique that can facilitate the location of wrecks of varying importance and sometimes the discovery of veritable archaeological treasures.

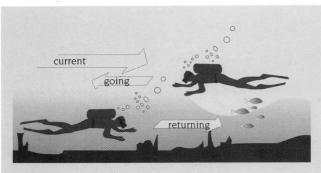

**DIVING PARTNER**
When diving on wrecks, a companion is an indispensable safety presence. When descending in groups, it is best to establish diving pairs (above).

**SUPPORT VESSEL**
A 13 inches diameter decompression cable (min. 30 feet);
B 13 pounds weight
C reserve air tank for decompression, sliding on the line
D weighted blackboard
E O2 cylinder with regulator or first aid kit with O2 and oro-pharyngeal mask
F boatman with experience in diver assistance
G line with snap hook
H VHF aerial

**GRAPNEL**
This is a tool consisting of a metal pipe or rod sprouting three or four metal barbs and connected to a sufficiently long cable (at least 1.5 times the depth of the water). It is lowered onto the seabed as the boat advances slowly in the search zone, and pulled in tow.

**SEABED SEARCH**
You descend along the anchor rope; when close to the bottom you must memorize its position so as to find it easily at the end of the dive. If the wreck is not visible, attach a cord to the anchor (Ariadne's thread) and radiate within a 65.6 feet circle.

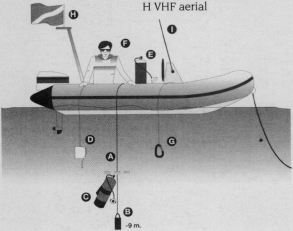

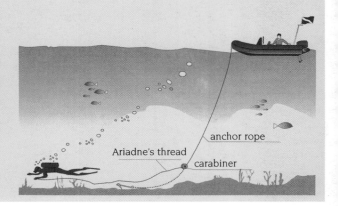

# Technique and equipment

Man first established a relationship with the underwater world through free-diving, using the natural air tank of his lungs to breathe. Over the centuries, however, free-diving equipment has developed, permitting easier movement in the marine environment. Each element of your equipment is vital, and, consequently, all pieces should be maintained and checked before every dive. Fins and a mask are certainly the free-diver's most important aids; a clear view of his or her surroundings is as important as being able to give a big kick to reach the desired depth with less effort. Professional free-divers use fins with very long blades for a stronger kick, but those who are not trying to break diving records should adopt less extreme fins, partly to avoid the risk of muscular cramps. The temperature of the water is a problem to be solved with a wetsuit, the density and thickness of which can, again, be more or less extreme depending on the environment. A compass, a knife, and a surface buoy complete the basic equipment.

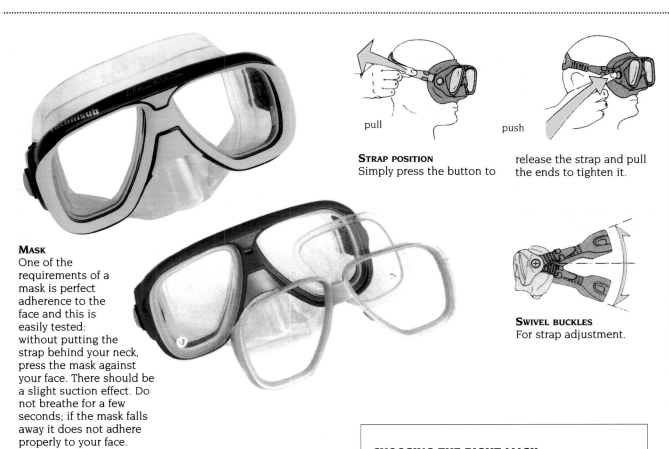

**STRAP POSITION**
Simply press the button to

release the strap and pull
the ends to tighten it.

pull

push

**SWIVEL BUCKLES**
For strap adjustment.

**MASK**
One of the requirements of a mask is perfect adherence to the face and this is easily tested: without putting the strap behind your neck, press the mask against your face. There should be a slight suction effect. Do not breathe for a few seconds; if the mask falls away it does not adhere properly to your face.

**COMPASS AND DEPTH GAUGE**
These instruments are needed to indicate the position and depth reached.

**KNIFE**
A multi-purpose tool. Materials of good quality are essential.

## CHOOSING THE RIGHT MASK

Of all the scuba diving equipment available, the mask would seem the easiest choice to make. Actually this is not so, partly because today's market offers a truly vast selection, allowing you to opt for the model best suited to your intended use and personal specifications. When buying a mask, try it on dry, in keeping with a classic procedure: rest it against your face and breathe in through your nose. If there is the usual suction effect, or rather if the mask "sticks" to your face, there will be no infiltration (air or water) when you are in the water.
This procedure seems fairly straight foward but take care, because in some dry situations, the mask may seem to hold but then underwater may not be totally hermetic. As a precaution, therefore, you should check that it sticks softly to your face and that your nose fits "comfortably" into the nose pocket. This latter aspect is important because if the mask is unconfortable or painful; you may not be able to wear it for long in the water. You should also check that the equalizing movement (Valsalva technique) is easy and automatic; that is, it must not be difficult to grasp and squeeze your nostrils from the outside of the mask. Lastly, visibility: the field of vision must be wide but not exaggerated; an overlarge mask has disadvantages, especially for free-divers. The angle of vision must be sufficiently large in proportion to the size of the mask.

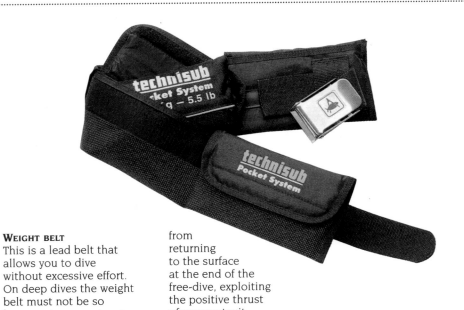

### WEIGHT BELT

This is a lead belt that allows you to dive without excessive effort. On deep dives the weight belt must not be so heavy as to prevent you from returning to the surface at the end of the free-dive, exploiting the positive thrust of your wetsuit.

### LIGHT

This is certainly an essential aid on night dives, in caves, or on a poorly illuminated seabed.

### WETSUIT

The competition free-diver's ideal wetsuit is of very fine thickness (0.09/0.13 inches) and is worn like a second skin. It is made from Neoprene and is extremely elastic. The thicker the suit the warmer it will be in the water.

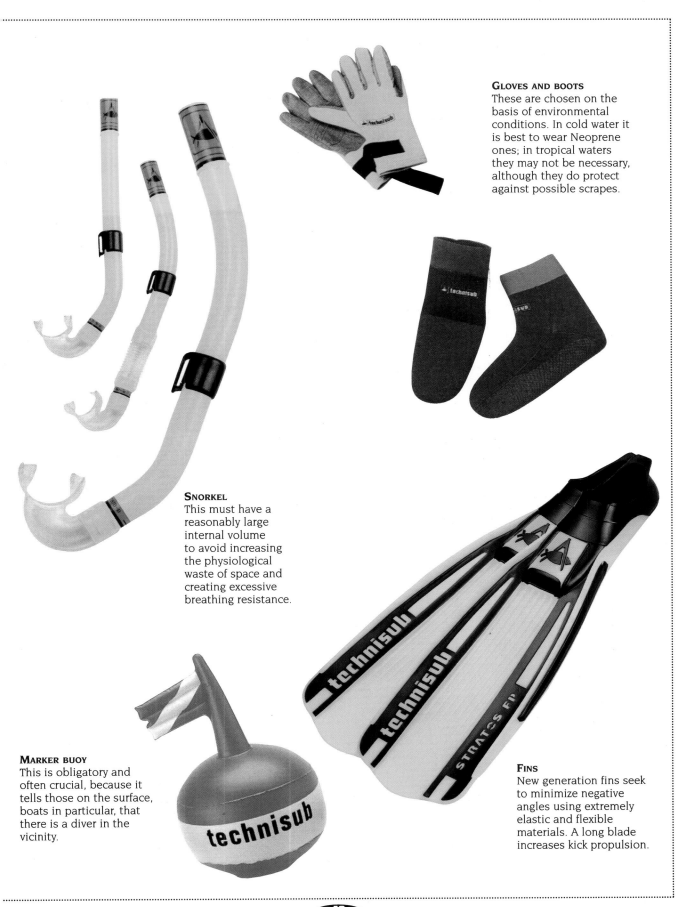

**GLOVES AND BOOTS**
These are chosen on the basis of environmental conditions. In cold water it is best to wear Neoprene ones; in tropical waters they may not be necessary, although they do protect against possible scrapes.

**SNORKEL**
This must have a reasonably large internal volume to avoid increasing the physiological waste of space and creating excessive breathing resistance.

**FINS**
New generation fins seek to minimize negative angles using extremely elastic and flexible materials. A long blade increases kick propulsion.

**MARKER BUOY**
This is obligatory and often crucial, because it tells those on the surface, boats in particular, that there is a diver in the vicinity.

# Entering the water

These swimming pool exercises are good preparation for subsequent free-diving outings. You start from the initial moment of entry into the water and gradually perfect sliding and, as a result, the movements that produce the hydrodynamic thrust.

**CORRECT INITIAL DIVE POSITION**
Note the way the knees are bent so that shoulders and feet are well aligned on the edge of the pool.

**ENTERING THE WATER**
Proceed with the active phase of the initial dive to actually enter the water. It is vital not to lose alignment: the head must be between outstretched arms and the feet extended. At this stage the most common error is to hold your head too high above your trunk, and to have your legs not perfectly aligned but open like scissors, with resulting loss of balance and hydrodynamics.

**SLIDING INTO THE WATER**
Left: the push will be good if the starting position is correct: good entry into the water with resulting slide. Avoid all sudden movements. It is important to strive for great fluidity and to feel at home in the water.

Right: the perfectly elongated position in the water highlights the correct exploitation of the push. The exercise is complete if you are able to swim without breathing for at least 98 feet.

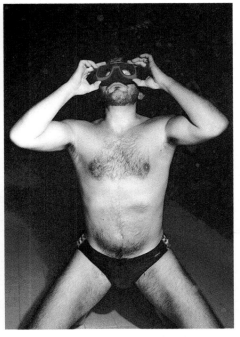

**TRAINING EXERCISE TO CLEAR MASK WITHOUT LOSING AIR**
This is done by calculating the quantity of air (left) that must be emitted to evacuate just the water from the mask (right). This exercise requires a more controlled movement than the mask clearing seen in the basic course. This is a specific preparation exercise for free-diving.

# Extreme free-diving

Free-diving, or apnoea, which etymologically means "without breathing," could be explained as the operation of holding your breath to reach the seabed from the surface. In extreme conditions, however, it becomes an attempt to establish personal limits and a challenge within an environment that is not natural to humans. Champion free-divers past and present all share the same passion for the sea, a methodical approach to training, and the checks to which they are subjected before they try to set a new diving record. One of the principal forms of training is to accustom the lungs to working at their maximum capacity, thus increasing their ability to store air. The operation that prepares the athlete for prolonged dives is called hyperventilation. This consists of breathing in and out a number of times, deeply and slowly, in order to store oxygen and reduce carbon dioxide to a minimum. This will delay, as much as possible, the desire to breathe. This exercise must be performed correctly, without exceeding certain limits. At the onset of symptoms such as "pins and needles" in the fingers and lips, and giddiness, the diver must start breathing normally again and refrain from diving.

### SEEKING PERSONAL LIMITS
There are two types of free-diving record attempts:

**1. variable ballast**
The diver uses a weight that must be abandoned the moment the he or she reaches the set depth before ascending again with the positive assistance of a wetsuit.

**2. constant ballast**
The diver must resurface with the same equipment used to descend. Often, although extreme, deep-diving attempts provide a vital opportunity to study free-diving limits and the stress to which a diver's body is subjected.

### UMBERTO PELIZZARI
is the most prestigious current representative of the extreme free-diving sector. Born in 1965, he has a lung capacity of 7 quarts. In 1984 he started to devote his time to competitive free-diving and he has, since then, attained a number of successes and records. On his debut, in November 1990, he set a new record for constant-ballast diving of -213 feet, taking it away from the Cuban Pipin Ferreras, who had set the record three months earlier. Within the space of a month in 1991, he set all the free-diving records: -220 feet in constant ballast, -312 feet in variable ballast, -387 feet in absolute variable ballast. In September 1997, he reached -377 feet in variable ballast. His last fascinating exploit was in September 1998, when he reached -328 feet without a wetsuit and without fins, assisting his descent with a 15 pound stone.

# The physiology of diving

During a free-dive or even just underwater, our bodies are subjected to considerable changes in pressure that affect the various organs and systems within it.

Heart and circulatory system: diving in water at temperatures generally lower than that of the air causes changes in the circulation. The small blood vessels just under the skin contract and the inner ones expand. The heart, subjected to increasing pressure, reacts by increasing its contractions and reducing the number of heartbeats.

Respiratory system: as the free-diver descends in depth two phenomena occur: the external hydrostatic pressure increases and the gas contained in the lungs decreases. At this stage, the blood tends to establish a "preferential circulation" flowing to the lungs, which therefore become practically incompressible and enriched with oxygen. This phenomenon is also known as "blood shift."

Brain: the organ that presides over all our body's functions is extremely sensitive to lack of oxygen; permanent damage may result if the brain is denied oxygen for more than three to four minutes. The hyperventilation technique used by free-divers reduces the size of the blood vessels causing a limited flow of blood. Overlong hyperventilation produces sensations similar to the loss of consciousness.

The drawing clearly illustrates the phenomenon of hydrostatic thrust, explained by Archimedes' Principle.

Opposite page: Gianluca Genoni, one of the world's most famous free-divers, is about to attempt a new record. After his success in competitive swimming as a boy, this Italian diver devoted himself totally to free-diving at the age of 20. In 1998 he set the world record in variable ballast, descending to a depth of -397 feet (Sardinia). His objective is -330 feet in variable ballast, a depth considered impossible by many experts. His records also include that of static free-diving at 7 min. and 30 seconds.

# Equalization

Our bodies contain a number of cavities filled with air. The difference in pressure between the water's surface and various depths has a definite impact on these cavities, particularly the sinus and ears. Our ear is made up of three parts: outer, middle, and inner ear. The auricle and external auditory canal make up the outer ear; the tympanic membrane and auditory ossicles form the middle ear; the labyrinth and cochlea make up the inner ear. The eustachian tube connects the middle ear to the pharynx and nose. The pressure exercised when diving becomes greater as the depth increases and, as a result,

the hydrostatic pressure on the eardrums must be equalized to avoid rupturing the eardrum. To do this, air must be introduced into the middle ear to balance the external and internal pressure. This is done by swallowing, Valsalva's procedure, and Marcante-Odaglia's procedure, this latter being used in particular by free-divers. Both procedures consist of pushing air from the pharynx into the middle ear through the eustachian tube. In the first case, the push comes from the lungs and diaphragm, in the second from the soft palate without affecting heart and lungs.

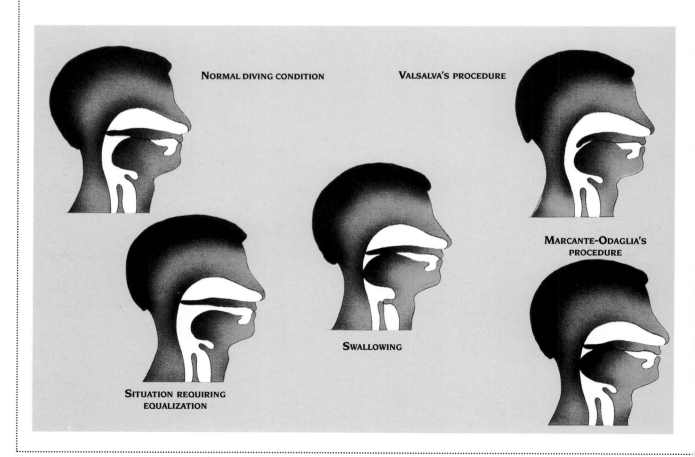

NORMAL DIVING CONDITION

VALSALVA'S PROCEDURE

MARCANTE-ODAGLIA'S PROCEDURE

SWALLOWING

SITUATION REQUIRING EQUALIZATION

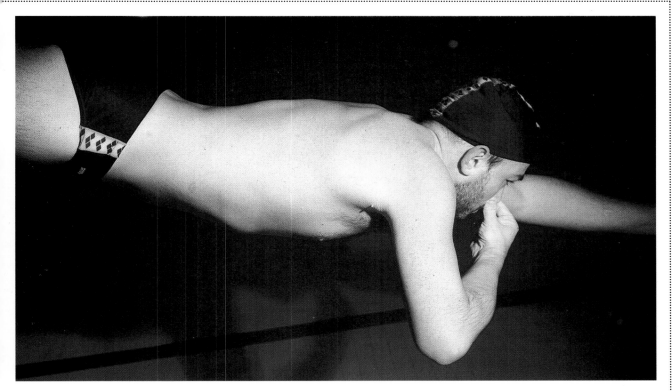

Learning how to equalize correctly is one of the main steps in a diver's training. To equalize, squeeze your nose and emit air as if you were trying to swallow. It is important to equalize repeatedly in the first few feet without waiting to feel pain in your eardrums.

Below: some divers practise equalising with equipment.

# Free-diving movements

A free-diver must always consider certain laws that govern the underwater environment if he is to exploit his or her abilities to the fullest. If a free-diver is to understand his or her own equilibrium and choose the right weight for the set descent, he or she must be familiar with Archimedes' Principle (the up-thrust to a body immersed in fluid is equal to the weight of fluid displaced), which governs the buoyancy of bodies and therefore of every diver underwater.

Naturally, if we are not concerned with deep free-diving, but merely swimming without breathing, certain aids become vital: fins, for example, which permit extensive fast movements without the consumption of too much precious oxygen. A free-diver can make long transfers along the surface to the area designated for deeper diving. Once underwater, movements must be slow and ample to gain the proper thrust, but without a wasteful excess of energy and, of course, of air reserves.

In dreams and legends, human beings are capable of living in the underwater world, moving and swimming like dolphins. These legends sometimes have roots in reality—witness the Polynesian fishermen who, under the water, move with the ease of the dolphins.

**DESCENT TO THE SEABED**
The next movement after the roll, or entry into the water, is the descent to the seabed (above left). This highlights the maximum use of hydrodynamic thrust. The limbs are in the correct position, perfectly aligned with the body for the smoothest descent.

Top Right: arm and leg movements must be coordinated to fully exploit the initial thrust. Bottom Right: ascent from the seabed without leg thrust. This useful exercise increases confidence and self-control. Remember that this is performed after a free-dive, when self-control is easily lost.

# Free-diving accidents

The principal problem that may be encountered by anyone diving without breathing equipment, either in a swimming pool or in the sea, is "syncope," or fainting. In the diving world, syncope means loss of consciousness with interrupted breathing (simple syncope) or, following this, a flooding of the airways and subsequent cardiac and circulatory arrest (complex syncope). This is usually divided into voluntary or direct syncope and involuntary or reflex syncope depending on its causes.

## VOLUNTARY SYNCOPE

Those wishing to put themselves to the test often go beyond their personal limits, making crucial errors, such as performing prolonged hyperventilation (voluntary syncope). This deadens our bodies' alarm signals and the person falls into syncope without realizing it. In this case, the syncope is caused by a lack of oxygen and excess carbon dioxide.

Another special case of syncope is "ascent syncope," which affects divers who remain too long in the water at a particular depth. During the ascent there is a sharp fall in absolute pressure and, therefore, also of the partial oxygen pressure, which in these cases reaches a level that prevents normal brain activity. There is a clash between the oxygen reduction and the increase in carbon dioxide, caused by the muscular effort made to emerge, and the diver falls into syncope.

## REFLEX SYNCOPE

Reflex syncope is provoked by a shock or a message sent by the nervous system. One of the most common is called "abdominal congestion," which may take a diver by surprise. It is marked by a greater flow of blood and hence oxygen to the digestive system. The nervous reaction caused by contact with water that is too cold reduces the flow of blood and oxygen, already scarce, to the other parts of the body provoking syncopal consequences.

## COMPLICATIONS

In the case of a diver affected by syncope with penetration of water into the airways, there is the risk of blood leaking into the alveoli and bronchi, resulting in eventual cardiac arrest. This is a life-or-death situation requiring immediate action.

---

**THE FREE-DIVER'S TEN DIETARY COMMANDMENTS**

1. Eat a varied and balanced diet.
2. Eat meals sitting down, within a reasonable space of time, perhaps three to four light meals a day.
3. Maintain a balanced diet during training.
4. Reduce the number of meals during competitions.
5. End a meal at least three hours before a dive.
6. Meals are to contain 60-70% in glucides, the rest in lipids and proteins.
7. Drink no alcohol on the day of the dive nor the day before.
8. After the dive, drink a sufficient amount of water (17 ounces).
9. The first meal after a dive must be light and contain few lipids and proteins.
10. The free-diver must maintain his or her optimum weight.

# Technique and equipment

Scuba diving is practiced with compressed air breathing apparatus, known as air tanks, a fundamental part of the equipment and essential to conduct operations underwater without experiencing breathing problems. Modern scubas date from the end of the Second World War, although history records many attempts and studies previously made. The ancient Romans used to dive with leather bags full of air and weighted. Every now and again they managed to supply themselves with air from these.

For many years, indeed centuries, numerous attempts were made to find a better solution, without considering the fact that it is impossible to breathe air underwater unless it is supplied at the same hydrostatic pressure as that to which the diver is subjected. In France, in 1933, the first independent breathing apparatus was created by Commander Le Prieur, followed later by what can be considered the true forebear of today's apparatus, which was perfected by Cousteau-Gagnan.

**FINS**
Scuba fins are short and wide with rubber blades.

**STABILIZERS**
Stabilizers are an extension of the foot pocket and offer major advantages: they transmit the effort made by the foot directly to the heart of the fin; they channel water to ensure that the fin has maximum stability and to eliminate the phenomenon of dérapage.

**BLADE**
This is made in layers of two materials, rubber and technopolymer.

**AIR TANK**
The tank is the container that stores compressed air and is made of special steel.

**REGULATOR**
This emits air at a pressure of between 8 and 14 bars. In this case the pressure is 9 bars.

**DIVER SIGNALING SYSTEM**
An end-of-dive signal approximately 59 inches long. A lead weight at the base of the signal keeps it vertical.

## MASK

The mask is fundamental. It may take optical lenses and must allow easy grip of the nose for comfortable equalizing.

## KNIFE

The knife must be strong and sharp.

## LIGHT

The light is an essential accessory for night dives or in areas of poor visibility such as caves or inside wrecks.

## GLOVES AND BOOTS

Gloves and boots serve as protection against water temperature and possible accidents.

## BUOYANCY COMPENSATOR

The buoyancy compensator allows a diver to counter what is known as Archimedes' thrust by introducing or removing air.

## HOW TO TEST YOUR WETSUIT

The best thing would be to test a new wetsuit in the water but as this is not always possible, there are some rules to follow when you purchase such an important complement to underwater activities. First of all, do not try on a new wetsuit if you have been perspiring. If necessary, use some talcum powder to make it easier to put on. Once you have the wetsuit on, crouch down on your knees to check for freedom of movement. If it tends to pull at any point it is not the right one. Raise your arms and stretch them forward. In doing so you will realize if there is any air intake under your armpits, which may come from the neck of the suit, the wrists, or even from the hood ring. The armpit area of the body must not absorb air as, in the water, this would mean storing air inside the suit with every movement of your body.

**WETSUIT**
The main function of the wetsuit is to protect the diver from the cold and also against possible abrasions or knocks. It is made from insulating material, Neoprene, and consists of jacket, hood, and pants.

# Jumping in

The entry into the water should be treated as the combination of several preliminary operations that are indispensable if you are to dive confidently and safely. First, check all equipment thoroughly and efficiently. Then, with your diving partner, plan all the passages required to reach the set objective. Always use a marker buoy unless a vessel with the proper flag is following operations from the surface. After all the checks are completed, the moment of jumping in arrives, which, if from a boat, can be either by the classic "step forward" or a "backward" entry. In both cases it is important to make sure that the air tanks and mask are in place. Once on the seabed, after due equalization, check that your partner is present and check your instrumentation.

**JUMPING IN**
(1) Before entering the water, a diver must check his equipment.
(2) He then puts it on and checks the adjustment of the straps, weightbelt, mask, and depth control gauges.
(3) Vertical entry: this is used when the jump from the pool or boat edge is more than 4.9 feet.
(4) Sitting roll: this
is an alternative to the above when the distance to the water is between 1 foot and 5 feet.

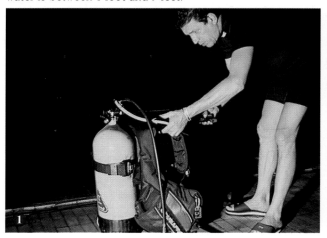

## REMOVING EQUIPMENT

(1) After entering the water the diver should equalize, holding the mask. (2) After acquiring a neutral position at the desired depth, established in advance, the diver moves horizontally to explore. In a supine position on the bottom of the pool, the diver prepares to remove the equipment (air tanks). This is an important exercise: movements must be precise and fluid. (3) With practice, they will gradually become automatic. The diver completes the exercise of removing the air tanks. To complete the exercise it is necessary to refit the equipment in the water. (4) This is a very important exercise because it helps to control breathing while maintaining a neutral position in the water. To gain stability the diver must bend the knee resting on the bottom of the pool while gripping with the other foot. (5) After removing the mask, the diver puts it on again and then clears it.

Opposite page: two divers on an open-water dive.

(1) Without tanks, the diver maintains position on the bottom of the pool. (2,3) A phase that precedes the refitting of the equipment. (4) The diver regains the position lost during the previous phase. (5) Completely re-equipped, with a regained neutral position, the diver can proceed to explore.

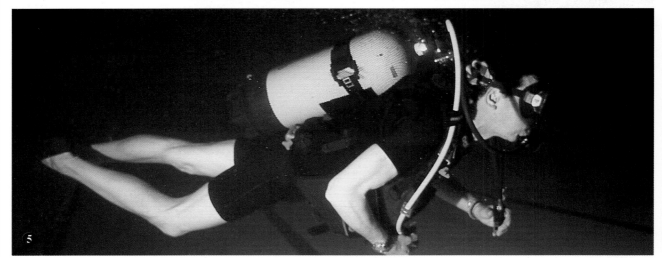

At last, it is time to dive in the open water and apply the techniques learned during courses in the swimming pool. Remember to carefully check all your equipment and confirm communication signals with your diving companion.

# Decompression

What is decompression? Air is a combination of gases: nitrogen, oxygen, and others present in smaller percentages. Although the body burns oxygen as fuel, nitrogen inhaled under pressure enters the blood and liquefies. If a diver full of liquefied nitrogen surfaces too quickly, the gas returns to the gaseous state too quickly and the blood is "invaded" by the resulting nitrogen bubbles trying to open a way for themselves—damaging the tissues, breaking veins and causing internal blisters. In the mildest of cases a diver feels itchy, in the worst the victim suffers atrocious pain, paralysis, and death. To avoid these potentially fatal effects, when ascending a diver must make decompression stops based on the time he or she has been under and the depth reached. Indications given by decompression tables state how many stops are required to return the body to its correct equilibrium.

**PLANNING A DIVE**
Certain rules must be respected to plan a safe dive:

a) maintain a descent speed of 33/50 feet per minute to allow the body to adapt to the new environmental conditions

b) the time spent is calculated from the beginning of the descent to the beginning of the ascent

c) time on the seabed: this is the period that a diver spends on the seabed, excluding descent and ascent

d) maintain ascent speed: 33 feet per minute to allow the nitrogen to evacuate the tissues correctly

e) decompression stop to be performed on a safety curve: one 3-minute stop at 10 feet.

# Underwater communication

**ALL OK**
This can be question and/or answer. As a question: when a diver wishes to inquire about the conditions of his diving partner. If all is well his companion responds with the same signal.

**OK ALL IS WELL**
Signal used when wearing gloves

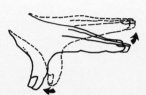

**NOT OK**
This is not used in an emergency and must be followed by the indication of what is wrong.

**COMMENCE ASCENT -
I AM COMMENCING ASCENT**
An order: if made by the head diver to the other divers. Information: when a diver intends to ascend.

**COMMENCE DESCENT -
I AM COMMENCING DESCENT**
Order: if made by the head diver.
Information: when a diver intends to descend.

**STOP WHERE YOU ARE**
This is the signal made by the head diver to another diver. It must be followed by a signal explaining what to do next.

**IMMEDIATE ASSISTANCE**
Emergency. This signal is made by a diver in distress.

**EMERGENCY**
This signal is made by a diver unable to open the reserve. The nearest diving companion must immediately open the reserve for him or her.

**I AM ON RESERVE**
Signal made by a diver to the head diver when opening the reserve.

**GET WITH YOUR BUDDY**

**YOU/I**
The index finger is pointed at the companion to whom the next signal is addressed.

**GO AHEAD,
I WILL FOLLOW**

**OK** ALL IS WELL, ON THE SURFACE FROM A DISTANCE

**ALL IS WELL ON THE SURFACE**
This signal must be made by every diver to the head diver when surfacing and then to the support vessel.

**OK** ALL IS WELL, ON THE SURFACE FROM A DISTANCE WHEN YOU HAVE ONE HAND BUSY

**DIFFICULTY—COME AND GET ME**
Signal made by a diver in difficulty (or assisting a diver in difficulty)—*slow movement*. Emergency. The same signal requests immediate help—*fast movement*.

**I** AM OUT OF BREATH
Emergency. Signal made by a diver to the head diver or the nearest diver to indicate an emergency state and request immediate suspension of the work/swimming in order to regain breathing rhythm.

**DANGER**
Emergency. Signal made by a diver who sees a source of danger and indicates the direction.

**NO MORE AIR**
Emergency. A diver making this signal requires immediate assistance sharing air.

**I** AM COLD

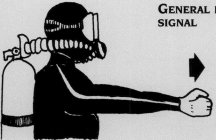

**GENERAL DANGER SIGNAL**

**I** CANNOT CLEAR MY EARS

# Shoals

A shoal is a special conformation of the seabed that due to its morphology impedes or complicates advancement. This is a sharp rise at any particular point regardless of its depth from the surface or its extension. These sometimes rise gradually, sometimes they are steeply vertical. Shoals are generally also found in open water and thanks to their currents they are extremely rich in life. Often they are interesting historical archives after boats run aground on them and become submerged relics. Because a shoal may "appear" suddenly in a stretch of open water, when diving it is essential to have a support boat and a reliable diving partner experienced in swimming on this type of seabed, able to follow attentively his partner's underwater bubbles. Safety measures must necessarily be adopted for all types of dives. In this specific case, the diver must always maintain contact with the support boat via the anchor rope, which will be used for ascent and for the fundamental 3-minute stop at a depth of 10 feet.

The drawing shows a typical seabed on which a higher area suddenly appears. Although this area represents a danger for boats, divers will most certainly find it an interesting exploration zone.

Before diving on a shoal, a diver should, indeed, must, research in detail the morphology of the desired area. There are now several sources available for this purpose—organized by the various official Diving Centers, some of which also provide Internet sites containing detailed information on dives and providing important data and references for the planning and organization of a safe dive. Because of the morphology of the seabed, shoals offer a rich variety of life forms, which vary according to the area being explored. A sandy bed may rise in a monolith full of cavities or be the beginning of a vertical descent of several meters with perhaps a chance to come across caves with fascinating interior routes.

# Scuba accidents

Undertaking a scuba dive is never dangerous if you have a good knowledge of the technical, physiological, and psychological difficulties to be expected. Accidents are sometimes caused by external factors, but most often by carelessness. One of the main accidents that a scuba diver can experience is decompression sickness (D.C.S.) or "the bends." This problem is linked to an ascent made too quickly without stopping for decompression to allow the nitrogen, previously liquefied in the blood, to return to its gaseous form and be expelled evenly and constantly.

D.C.S. symptoms can be divided into general, local, and serious.

**General:** abdominal, lumbar, and chest pain, shock.

**Local:** itching, rashes, and painful joints.

**Serious:** paralysis of one or more limbs, vision problems, loss of consciousness, respiratory and cardiac arrest, crushing feeling in the chest, heart palpitations. Another problem that may occur with scuba equipment is nitrogen narcosis, the effects of which are similar to those produced by too much alcohol. This may be experienced at shallow depths, causing strange reactions (irrational behavior, loss of direction, attempts to ascend to the buoy), or at deep depths, where the narcotic syndrome has far more lethal effects. It will lead to a loss of consciousness if the diver is unable to regain control. The last, quite serious accident is traumatic embolism, caused by a very fast and uncontrolled ascent. The possible reasons for this are many, including a blocked regulator and the need to make a free ascent, exploiting the air in the lungs. Remember air will double in volume in the last 33 feet.

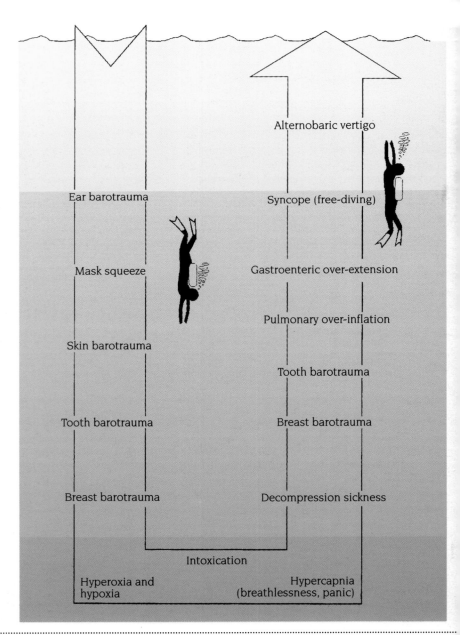

Alternobaric vertigo

Ear barotrauma — Syncope (free-diving)

Mask squeeze — Gastroenteric over-extension

Pulmonary over-inflation

Skin barotrauma

Tooth barotrauma

Tooth barotrauma — Breast barotrauma

Breast barotrauma — Decompression sickness

Intoxication

Hyperoxia and hypoxia — Hypercapnia (breathlessness, panic)

NITROX

# Technique and equipment

Nitrox features the use of a special air mixture (also known as hyper-oxygenated), which is different from that used with standard scuba and closed circuit equipment.

Diving with Nitrox allows a diver to remain underwater quite a long time without having to make decompression stops. More specifically it adopts two basic mixtures: Nitrox I, with an oxygen content equal to 32%, and Nitrox II, with an oxygen content of 36%. These percentages have been fixed and regulated by the National Oceanic and Atmospheric Administration. The two standard mixtures are suited to two different uses: the first (32%) is suitable for traditional recreational use (dives with Nitrox to a maximum depth of 131 feet), the second (36%) is used for repetitive dives at shallower depths, but in some cases to 111.5 feet.

First stage of the **regulator-pressure** reducer.

Second stage delivers air at a pressure of between 8 and 14 bars. In this case the pressure is 9 bars.

**GAUGE**
A metal, high precision underwater hose gauge with fluorescent face. Operating depth: 328 feet.

**A BACK-MOUNTED BUOYANCY COMPENSATOR** with air positioned on the diver's back. This permits greater thrust with the same volume, no bulk at the front, and freedom to inflate the jacket without pressure points on the diver's body.

**DIAPHRAGM DEPTH GAUGE** with a parabolic 0–262 feet scale. A needle indicates the maximum depth reached.

**STEEL ALLOY AIR TANK WITH CHROME MOLYBDENUM** Internal anti-corrosion treatment. External protection guaranteed by hot galvanizing.

## LIGHT
This is essential during dives. Rear grip ensures optimum efficiency and drastically reduces wrist stress.

## GLOVES
Gloves play an important part in a diver's equipment. They offer protection against stinging creatures and certain species of sponges, but also against rocks and coral that should never be grasped.

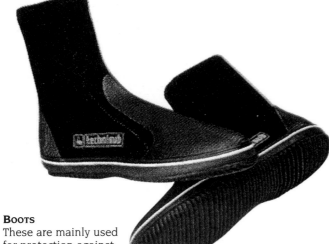

## BOOTS
These are mainly used for protection against the cold and are essential with strapped fins, usually in Neoprene, which are considered standard when diving with heavy equipment.

## WETSUIT
Neoprene has been used to make wetsuits in various shapes and colors for some time now. Some suits feature two linings, in an overall thickness that generally varies between 0.1 and 0.2 inches. The choice of thickness depends on the type of diving activity and the water temperature. Modern wetsuits have non-through seams and a particularly attentive design. Neoprene serves a diver's "second skin" but the most important factor to be considered when choosing a wetsuit is fit, which must be perfect.

**KNIFE**
Special stainless steel
blade.

**MASK**
The mask is essential and
may take optical lenses.
It must be easy to grip the
nostrils through the mask
for simple equalization.

**FINS**
The finning stroke has
two stages, positive and
negative. During the
positive phase, the water is
pushed backward as a duck
does with its webbed foot.
In the negative phase,
the recovery phase, the
diver must overcome the
resistance of the water.
The ends of the fins must
therefore yield under the
resistance of the water.

# Basic course

Nitrox, in various compositions, was first used by military forces as an alternative to standard scuba equipment during the First World War, as it permitted safe "secret" dives for spying on military and submarine action. Subsequently, the mixture was adopted in professional spheres by specialist underwater operators and scientific divers. N.O.A.A. studied how to create a mixture also suited to recreational use and has set legal limits for safe mixtures. In 1979, after nine years' study and the passing of precise regulations, Nitrox officially became a mixture for recreational purposes. There is a manual that governs the logistical aspects and, above all, two standard tables that define the two mixtures (32% and 36%). Nowadays, there is a whole range of equipment, such as Oli-Free compressors, portable O2 analyzers, and underwater computers. In Europe, Nitrox was first used for speleological diving and then became a niche specialization that is now fashionable and widely taught. The depth limit, fixed for safe regulation, coincides with the basic philosophy of traditional recreational underwater activity.

As well as important theoretical training (mental and operational flexibility), the basic Nitrox course includes some practical tests in the water. These pictures show a group about to undertake their first dive. These are dives in safety curves of depths not exceeding 131 feet. After an extensive review of the theory involved, the instructor usually performs a couple of test dives. Analysis of the mixture is thoroughly explained in the preliminary phases. It is very important to learn all about the special equipment and to be well aware of the standard registration procedures at the Recharging Centers.

# Diver safety

Recreational divers fall into one of several categories: those undertaking underwater trips for pleasure, instruction, or training; those using open-circuit scubas; and those staying within time and depth limits that do not require stops for decompression, generally less than 98 feet. The conditions experienced by recreational divers differ greatly from those of professional divers and therefore are not comparable. Recreational divers do not use equipment that reguires re-supplying on the surface; they do not make dives that require stops for decompression, diving bells, or desaturation techniques; they do not use tools, explosives, or underwater welding and cutting equipment. They do not go out in adverse weather or less than optimum diving conditions. Recreational divers choose a relatively shallow location suited to the purpose of the dive. When conditions become unsuitable or dangerous the recreational diver is trained to interrupt the dive immediately.

All the professional diver-training organizations have developed precise guidelines and a code of conduct. This helps a recreational diver make the appropriate choice and decide on the necessary safety precautions for that diving location. Places chosen and declared safe must have been "tested" in the previous ten years.

Statistics drawn up by American groups that have a long history in underwater activities prove that the percentage of underwater diving accidents has fallen considerably since recreational training agencies have grown and developed. This is due principally to the fact that recreational diving now means diving without decompression to reasonable depths in a spirit that is truly enjoyable and fun. Finally, scuba diving within accepted limits and regulations has proved itself safer than many other traditional sports such as skiing or swimming. In short, the R.S.T.C. supports dives without decompression to a maximum depth of 131 feet and is considered the international reference body for all coun- tries that have decided to regulate scuba diving properly and safely, whether for recreation or otherwise.

A Diving Center cannot be considered such unless it has an efficient recharging station for scuba tanks.

The table shows the values of the air components put into tanks according to American standards.

| ELEMENT | VALUE ALLOWED |
|---|---|
| OXYGEN | 20–21% |
| CARBON DIOXIDE | MAX. 0.1% |
| CARBON MONOXIDE | MAX. 0.002% |
| OIL VAPORS | MAX. 130 MICROGRAMS |
| HUMIDITY | 0% |
| DUST | 0% |

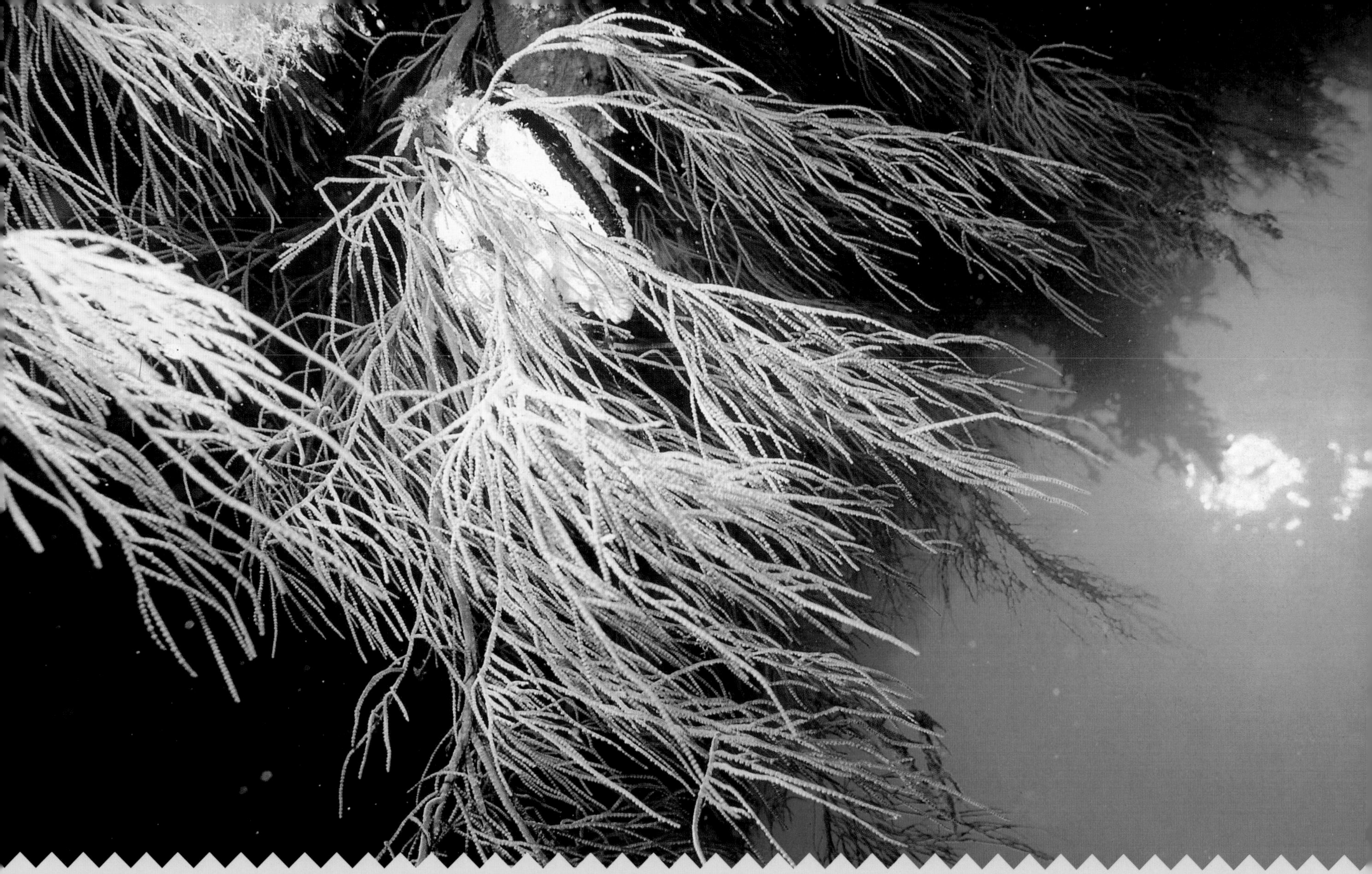

# CLOSED-CIRCUIT DIVING

# Technique and equipment

Closed-circuit oxygen equipment was created for military purposes because it does not give away the presence of a diver with the traditional tell-tale bubbles on the surface. The first oxygen breathing apparatus was made in 1911 by Sir Robert Davis. In 1930 Italy acquired the manufacturing rights, and closed-circuit apparatus was used on a huge scale during the Second World War by navy incursors, those who used the famous "pigs," technically called slow-advancing torpedoes. The difference between scuba and closed-circuit diving can be explained as follows: the former uses an open-circuit function (air is taken from a tank, sent at environmental pressure to the lungs and then discharged into the surrounding water); in the latter case, there is a semi-closed or closed circuit in which the air exhaled can be entirely or partially "reconditioned." As this is a technically complex type of apparatus, it must only be used after a specific training course and dives made, if possible, with a partner equipped with compressed air. It is advisable never to dive to depths in excess of 33 feet, nor for more than 45 minutes; and to always dive with a line.

Thanks to this apparatus a diver can breathe a gas (oxygen) or a gaseous mixture (compressed air) in order to maintain regular vital functions. Breathing apparatus come in three types: open, closed, or semi-closed circuits.
Open circuit is when the quantity of gas used with every breath is expelled into the external environment.
Closed circuit is when, with every breath, a certain amount of gas or gaseous mixture is ventilated; when exhaled it travels inside the apparatus where it is filtered and regenerated.
Semi-open or semi-closed circuit apparatus recovers a large or small quantity of the gas exhaled each time; the remainder is dispersed into the external environment.

The closed-circuit apparatus can supply a mixture at environmental pressure and eliminate the carbon dioxide exhaled from the mixture, guaranteeing a partial pressure of oxygen within breathable limits. The breather bag that receives the exhaled air is sensitive to environmental pressure and enables a diver to re-inhale the exhaled air. The air is channeled through a corrugated hose with a mouthpiece into a scrubber unit containing a mixture of soda lime. This absorbs the carbon dioxide exhaled and the same corrugated hose enables the diver to recycle the gas present in the breather bag. The oxygen tank restores the quantity of oxygen consumed.

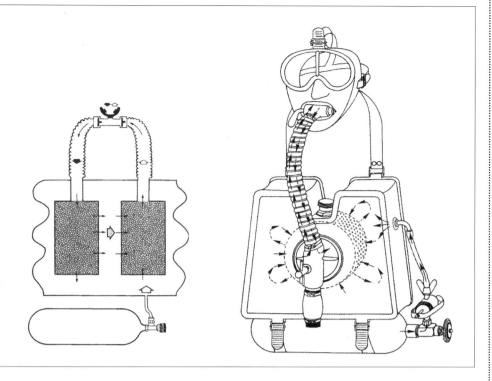

**THE FULL FACE MASK**
A typical part of rebreather equipment is this mask, used with closed-circuit apparatus. Unlike traditional masks, it features a direct attachment between mask and breather bag via a corrugated rubber hose connected to the mouthpiece. This is inserted directly into the mask.

**REBREATHING EQUIPMENT**
As well as a full face mask, closed-circuit equipment consists of an oxygen tank, breather bag, and a corrugated hose with mouthpiece.

# Diving

Closed-circuit apparatus requires more training and the most scrupulous teaching of all diving activities. The first rule to observe is the universal one of never diving alone and, even then, always remaining in constant communication with the surface. It should be stressed that the rules of the various boards and organizations involved in the use of closed-circuit apparatus (banned in some countries such as Great Britain) prohibit diving without a safety line and without surface guidance. After all the equipment has been fitted and the initial scrubbing operations performed, you enter the water with a vertical dive or a roll from the edge of the boat. The descent must be made slowly and calmly, activating the bypass at intervals so that fresh oxygen flows into the breather bag, to compensate for the reduction in volume caused by the gradually increasing hydrostatic pressure.

Rebreathing must be slow, deep, and regular because quickened breathing, with too fast a rhythm, may lead to breathlessness and does not allow the soda lime in the filter to complete its cycle of carbon dioxide filtering. The safety line must always be kept taut for constant contact in water, but it must not be too stretched as this will tire the diver. The main closed-circuit safety condition is that a boat on the surface must follow the diver. Aside from those piloting the boat, there should be present a group leader who remains in contact with the diver via the line and can monitor every stage of the dive. Using conventional signals via the line, this leader can feel the diver and perceive his or her movements. If diving in pairs, the second diver is connected to the first by a length of line between 7 and 16 feet long, depending on the requirements of the dive. The first diver must communicate directly with the surface and also remain in visual contact with the co-diver. The second diver is reciprocally monitoring the first diver, so that in case of need or danger, he or she may move to the safety line and communicate directly with the surface on behalf of the first diver.

## SAFETY

There are some essential rules that reduce risk factors in closed-circuit diving. A diver's sensitivity to oxygen must be considered as this varies from one person to another. Another important factor to be assessed, case by case, is the diver's physical fitness and psychological state. Two further basic conditions must be considered: the type of underwater work and the temperature of the water. You must learn to monitor yourself constantly and abstain from diving if you are physically or psychologically unwell.

### THE ESSENTIAL RULES OF REBREATHING ARE:

—Dive with expert partners and with a guide watching on the surface, or a diving companion equipped with compressed air.
—Always dive with a line, although keep in mind that a line does not eliminate all risks.
—Correctly perform the scrubbing operations (every 10 – 15 minutes); inhale gas from the breather bag through a mouthpiece and exhale through your nose.
—Do not perform these scrubbing operations through the three-way regulator.
—Never dive to depths of more than 33 feet.
—Never dive for longer than 45 minutes.
—Breathe slowly and deeply, pausing 4 or 5 seconds between inhaling and exhaling.

—Use a full face mask as often as possible because this avoids the loss of the mouthpiece and easy vocal signaling to co-divers.
—Alternate every 15 or 20 minutes of oxygen rebreathing with 5 minutes of compressed-air breathing.
—Complete equipment should include: full face mask, wetsuit, fins, weightbelt, depth gauge, watch, and knife.
—Check your equipment before every dive: oxygen cylinder load pressure, breather bag, soda lime, straps.
—Agree in advance with your co-diver or guide on: signals, diving times, maximum depth, dive leader, distance to be maintained between divers.
—Descent to the desired depth must be slow, introducing oxygen into the bag regularly to compensate for the reduction in volume caused by the increased pressure.
—On the seabed, keep the apparatus inflated at its correct value maintaining its proper position.
—Avoid overpressure or bag suction as they make breathing difficult.
—Avoid variations in depth because when ascending you would then be forced to constantly discharge oxygen externally to compensate for the increased volume—with the undesired result of decreasing autonomy.
—Ascent must be slow and controlled; compensate for the increased breather bag volume by discharging gas externally.

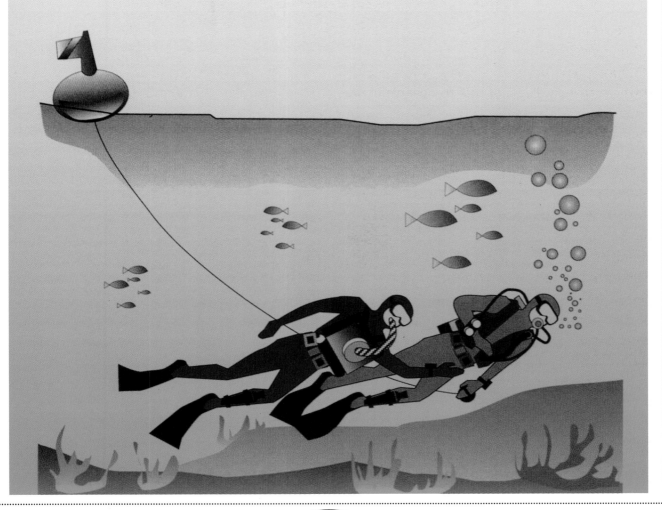

# Rebreathing problems

Although assuming that closed-circuit use is related to special dives and mainly practiced by specialists, problems may arise and these should be explained. Apart from the detailed lists of the risks that any technically complex activity presents, it should be remembered that dives must always be made with expert co-divers equipped with compressed air. Always dive with a line and with a support expert on a boat or contact point on the surface. Correctly perform the closed-circuit apparatus scrubbing operations. Never dive to depths of more than 33 feet or for more than 45 minutes. Always breathe slowly and deeply, and the ascent must also be slow and controlled, compensating for the increased volume of the breather bag by discharging gas externally.

## MECHANICAL PROBLEMS

- Loss of the mouthpiece because of a knock or overpressure in the breather bag.
- Ripping the breather bag on a sharp object.

## PHYSIOLOGICAL PROBLEMS

- Hyperoxia, or excessive increase of oxygen in the blood due to increased partial oxygen pressure.

- Hypoxemia, or excessive reduction of oxygen in the blood due to failure to scrub the breather bag.

- Hypercapnia, or increase in the quantity of carbon dioxide in the blood, which may occur for various reasons (physical tiredness, hastened ventilation, soda lime exhausted).

- Soda lime burns caused by inhaling the products of chemical reactions between soda lime and water.

- Anoxemia is the most serious form of hypoxemia and means a total absence of oxygen in the respiratory system.

- Breathlessness is in itself the most banal of difficulties a diver may encounter, but also the probable source of major dangers if not corrected in time with breathing returned to normal.

- Carbon dioxide poisoning is signaled by accelerated breathing rhythms that are also increased in degree; a headache and dulling sensation may also follow.

# Night diving

On night dives it is extremely important to be able to draw the attention of your co-diver when you need to communicate. This is done with short, frequent light signals produced by covering the light with your hand, not by using the switch to avoid damage to it or the bulb.

The signals shown in these pages have been divided into three basic groups:

—**INDICATION, COMMUNICATION, REQUEST**

—**WARNING, BEWARE, REQUEST**

—**EMERGENCY, URGENT REQUEST, ASSISTANCE**

**NIGHT SIGNALS**

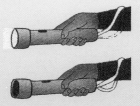

**Attacting attention**

**OK all is well**

**Come quickly – Emergency – Help**

## OK ALL IS WELL SIGNALS

Left: underwater

Right: on the surface

## DANGER SIGNALS

Left: all is not well

Center: request for help
on the surface

Right: danger underwater

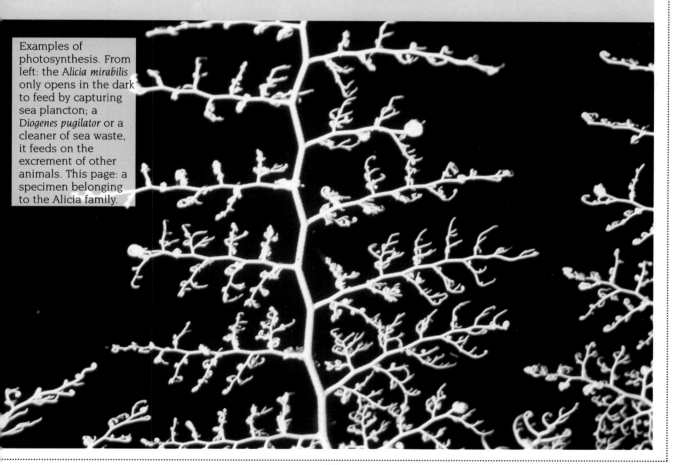

Examples of photosynthesis. From left: the *Alicia mirabilis* only opens in the dark to feed by capturing sea plancton; a *Diogenes pugilator* or a cleaner of sea waste, it feeds on the excrement of other animals. This page: a specimen belonging to the Alicia family.

# Wrecks

Archaeological research can often be very demanding and those involved must have a perfect knowledge of both the technical equipment and their own limits. The Mediterranean takes the prize for containing the richest archaeological treasures. Many ancient civilizations lived on the shores of this sea, their cargo ships often sank on the western and eastern coasts.

One of the world's oldest and most diverse wrecks lies on the seabed of Yassi Ada, on the Mediterranean coast of Turkey—200 copper ingots, 900 amphoras, gold coins, bronze scales bearing the name of the captain, silver bracelets and ivory—all from a Byzantine ship that came to rest at a depth of approximately 187 feet.

Another lovely diving point for archaeological divers is in the bay of Villefranche-sur-Mer, off the French Cote d'Azur: an Italian ship, which dates from around 1500. These are a few examples of wrecks to explore, it is up to you to discover the others.

Opposite page: a diver about to ascend and make his decompression stop.

A diver has just discovered a machine gun, a relic from a wreck on the seabed near Ponza, Italy. This is a landing craft dating from the Second World War.

One of the most famous wrecks in the world, the *Thistlegorm*, attracts numerous divers to depths of 59 to 101 feet. This is an English cargo ship that sank during an air bombardment in October 1941. It lies in the Gobal strait between the Sha'ab Abu Nuhas reef and the Sinai coast. Its size is impressive: the space that once held 9 thousand tons of cargo today provides refuge to the most varied sea inhabitants. This is a popular destination for enthusiasts of both history and marine biology. This dive calls for a medium – high preparation even though visibility is quite good and details are easily photographed.

Lying beside the famous *Thistlegorm* are two engines that came detached as it sank. The objects discovered by the diver (opposite bottom) were found inside the wreck, as was this old motorcycle (bottom). The area is also of interest for the presence of numerous other wrecks, for example, the *Ghiannis* D. (left), a modern cargo ship that sank just over ten years ago and lies alongside the *Thistlegorm*. This is thought to have been launched originally from a Japanese shipyard because of the wording (Shoyo Maru) discovered thanks to the corrosive action of the salt water. It lies at a depth of between 75 and 89 feet.

# Under the ice

Diving under the ice combines three different types of dive. Frozen lakes are found at certain altitudes and the diver may have to cope with the problems of high-altitude diving.

Environmental constriction under water and difficulty in movement makes the experience under the ice similar to that in caves. Lastly, the absorption of light may create situations similar to those of night diving.

The first major factor when planning a dive under the ice is the choice of the lake and where to make camp. Access to the lake is fundamental because you must avoid excessive effort after a dive in these conditions.

For safety reasons the divers delimit the area where they will make the dives. The most tiring job is that of making holes in the ice, which must be at least $4\frac{1}{2} \times 7$ feet each.

Once the ice plug has been cut, it is shifted with straps and levers, but left within the lake's perimeter because after the dive the holes are re-closed and marked with flags.

Usually gas-powered chainsaws are used to cut the ice and the blade must be longer than the thickness of the ice to avoid wasting time and energy. To make sure it works properly plan for the use of a heat source, as the saw's carburator may freeze at low temperatures. Once the ice plugs are cut, special ropes or straps are used to shift them and metal pipes or trunks to insulate them. At this stage the underwater route must be decided. Ropes will be required to define it vertically and cables to mark the route. Also required are weights for the vertical ropes plus fixing stakes and snap hooks.

The safety material required is: stakes and colored ribbons to mark off the field of action; wooden reinforcement to protect the corners of the holes; ropes to fix the planks; a means to facilitate entry and exit from the water; and ropes for the Ariadne's safety thread.

Protection planks are placed around the holes with the descent and ascent equipment. Once the equipment has been check and the divers fitted up, the dive can begin, which must necessarily be done in pairs. On this type of dive, reference marks are crucial, usually ropes linked to the surface and, in particular, an Ariadne's thread. This, with the use of conventional signals, becomes the diver's only means of communication with the surface.

Certain under-ice dives require the fitting of the air tanks after the diver has entered the water. After checking the connections and the safety ropes the two divers can start their excursion beneath the ice. All movements must have been agreed in advance by the pair. The use of a light in this case is fundamental.

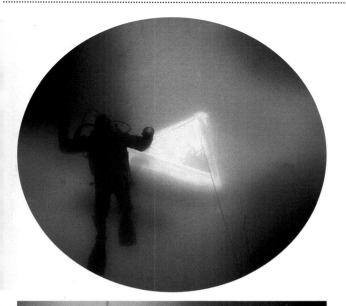

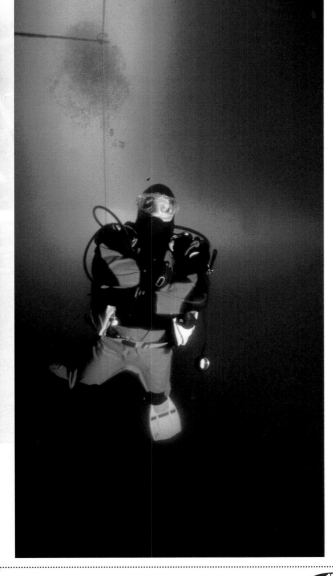

One of the crucial moments during a dive under ice is connecting the holes. A rescuer's intervention may be requested by the dive leader if, for instance, the original diving pair are late emerging from the water. The rescuer is connected to the end of a rope with a snap hook; the other end of the rope is secured to a stake in the ice. The length of the rope defines the range of action. A search is conducted in concentric circles, which are enlarged upward each time. It is essential on this type of dive to make frequent safety changes between the fitted divers waiting. This particular type of dive requires specific body training that should not be underestimated. A diver must be prepared to cope with the extreme cold before, during, and after the dive. Critical factors are calories consumed and the digestibility of food eaten.

# Terminology

• **Advanced open-water license**
Qualification to dive to a maximum depth of 131 feet without decompression stops.

• **Air tank**
Metal cylinder used to transport compressed gases.

• **Alcyonaria**
Members of the coelenterate family, an order represented by small polyps with a calcareous skeleton that live in colonies and often present bright, distinctive colorings.

• **Apnoea**
Temporary suspension of breathing.

• **Archaeological diving**
A special branch of archaeology devoted to the study of underwater relics. Special training is required.

• **Ariadne's thread**
A technical term used in dives under ice or for search and recovery. This is a safety connection used with conventional signals, which becomes the only means of communication between the diver and the surface or support boat.

• **Basic license**
Qualification to dive to a depth of 16 feet within a safety curve.

• **Blade**
The part of the fins that is crucial for thrust. There are various shapes and sizes for different uses.

• **Bowline**
This is the name for one of the most commonly used knots in the marine environment.

• **Breather bag**
Used in closed-circuit diving, this is the apparatus that receives the exhaled air and allows it to be recycled. It is connected directly to the full face mask by a corrugated hose.

• **Buoyancy compensator**
A buoyancy jacket that contrasts the Archimedes' thrust.

• **Butterfly knot**
A type of marine knot, specific for a point of attachment fixed with a loop.

• **Chlorophyll photosynthesis**
A fundamental biological process by which plants, supplied with chlorophyll, convert light energy into chemical energy.

• **Closed-circuit diving**
Done with closed-circuit breathing apparatus. Used within 33 feet, principally in the military field.

• **Constant ballast**
Descent and ascent with one's own forces with no variation in the diving equipment.

• **Coral reef**
Chain of rocks made of the calcareous skeletons of madrepore anthozoa in unpolluted water having a temperature of more than 64,4 °F, stable salinity, and extremely luminous conditions.

• **Corals**
Marine coelenterate anthozoa. Usually a polyp that lives in colonies and secretes a calcareous polyp colony, branched red, rose–colored and white. They live in warm seas.

• **Decompression**
The passage from one state of atmospheric pressure to a lower one.

• **Decompression table**
Fundamental aids on a dive, these are usually plastic-coated for easy use underwater. F.I.A.S. adopts that used by the U.S. Navy.

• **Depth gauge**
The instrument that tells a diver the depth reached in meters.

• **Diver signaling system**
An essential dive aid, a lead weight at the bottom holds the special end of dive signal vertical.

• **Ecosystem**
A combination of living beings, environment, physical and chemical conditions within a limited space.

• **Fitting up**
A fundamental procedure and decisive for the success of every dive.

• **Full face mask**
Typically used on closed-circuit dives and with an oxygen breathing system. The mask is directly connected to the breather bag.

• **Gorgonians**
Coelenterate that forms bushy, multi-colored colonies, typically found on a warm seabed.

• **Grapnel**
A claw used when diving on wrecks; this is connected to a rope and lowered onto the seabed in the search area and towed.

• **Hydrospeed**
This is practically a river bobsled; when equipped with wetsuit, fins and mask, you can dive with this and follow river courses. This sport was born and developed in France.

• **License**
Qualification at various levels acquired at the end of an approved course.

• **Madrepores**
Marine coelenterates that live in colonies and have a calcareous external skeleton; common mainly in the Red Sea and Indian Ocean where they create extensive rock formations.

• **Marker buoy**
An obligatory diving signal, this indicates to boats that there is a diver in the area.

• **Mask clearing**
A basic exercise practiced during the learning phase in the swimming pool, specific to the preparation of free-diving activities.

• **Neoprene**
A synthetic rubber used to make diving garments.

• **Nitrox**
A gaseous mixture composed of nitrogen and oxygen.

• **Ocean trench**
A depression on the seabed that registers maximum depths.

• **Open-water license**
Qualification to dive to a maximum depth of 98 feet within a safety curve.

*continued on p. 126*

# The Oceans

A boat, the lulling motion of the sea, reflections on the water, donning your wetsuit, the heavy scuba—a moment—you concentrate, then you dive. In just a few seconds the water engulfs you, drawing you into yet another adventure. You have entered the sixth continent: the sea. Whether diving for work or pleasure, you experience the moment your body becomes a part of the underwater world. The water, be it tropical, warm and crystal clear, or rough and stormy, is a magical place, as well as an arena for challenging personal limits. The ocean is the vast expanse of water that surrounds the continents: a horizontal and vertical immensity. The vast sea is incredibly iverse—from coral reefs to the atolls in the Pacific; from the sinister and alluring ice mountains in Greenland and Patagonia to the slowly undulating Red Sea or Indian Ocean; from the crystalline reflection of the sea around Sardinia to the variegated seabed of the Mediterranean Sea. For anyone drawn to the sea, the opportunity is an indescribable experience, like the sensation savored when from the seabed you look up at the surface as you start to ascend. Dreams and adventure need not be found only in distant paradises; discovery awaits those who want to explore their own regions, as well as dedicate themselves to maintaining the beauty and purity of their home waters.

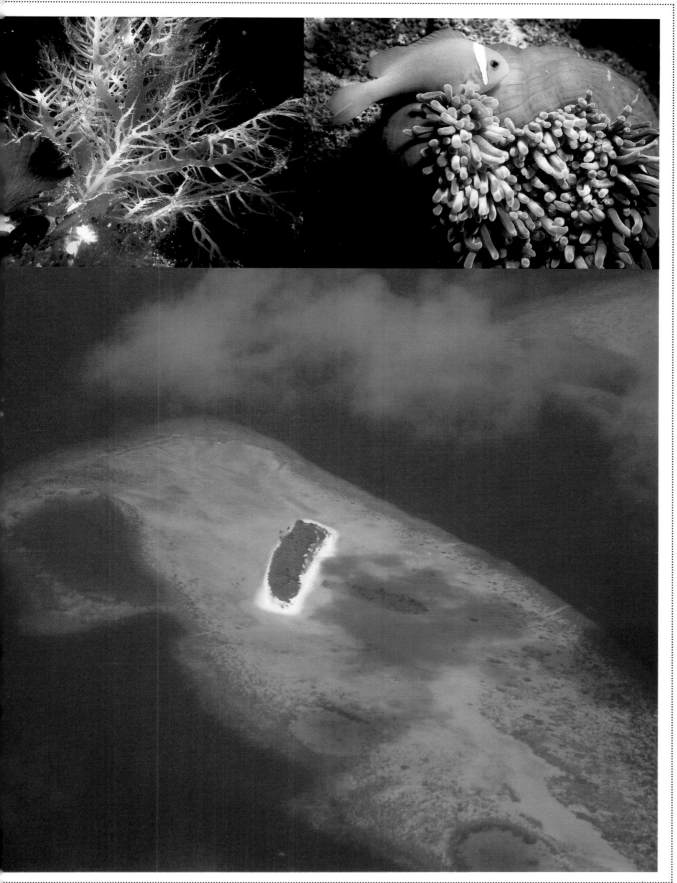

The chance to dive in natural habitats with diverse characteristics, an encounter with a sperm whale, for example, is the good fortune of divers entering the waters of the Azores in the Atlantic Ocean.

In the heavenly Seychelles of the Indian Ocean one may spy Red Sea corals and gorgonians; or in the waters around the Polynesian atolls one may explore coral reefs with the chance of meeting a shark.

# Red Sea

Although called the Red Sea, to scuba diving enthusiasts it is actually the "sea of colors." The only problem is choosing where to dive, as there really is something for everyone. Not surprisingly, diving centers have blossomed quickly, especially in the last decade, and humble fishing villages along the coast of the famous Sharm el Sheikh and Hurghada in Egypt have given way to large hotels and well-equipped holiday resorts. The diving centers in these parts are certainly among the most advanced in the training of guides and scuba instructors, and all scuba activities (Nitrox included) can be practiced. They are also the most suitable places for amateurs who can nevertheless snorkel effortlessly and find themselves surrounded by myriad colorful fish. A paradise such as the famous underwater park of Ras Mohammed is known as the "sanctuary of Allah," whereas Hurghada has become a favorite destination for lovers of wreck and archaeological diving. Flights travel via Khartoum to Port Sudan, the dream destination of divers all over the world. Direct flights (with charter flights available, too) link well-known resorts such as Sharm el Sheikh and Hurghada in Egypt and Eilat in Israel, which is famous for its coral gardens. Local airports feature shuttle transfers to the resorts of Safaga and El Quseir, where the dives are almost as spectacular as those of the marvelous Sudan. For holidays with continuous diving there are the 130 Dahlak islands on the Eritrean coast.

Left, top: a *Pomacanthus*.
Center: a *Ciona intestinalis*, a typical Red Sea sponge.
Bottom: a *Cionidae*.
Opposite page: a *Torpedo marmorata*; this gentle giant of the sea feeds only on plankton and can weigh up to lbs. 661.

Above: an *Affinis*, which belongs to the Opisthobranchiate family.
Center: a tropical grouper.
Bottom: a common inhabitant of Red Sea waters.

# Maldives

Scuba divers are particularly fond of the nineteen atolls in the Maldives where at a depth of just a few meters they can meet large fish. Contact with these giants of the sea is thrilling, whether gentle turtles or Pacific whale sharks. Malé is the logistic base for all the divers in the world; not surprisingly some have transplanted themselves there to explore the atoll paradises. Extremely popular are the outings for enthusiasts of photography and videography, who find in the Maldives subjects for extraordinary pictures. Spectacular, but only recommended for expert or accompanied scuba divers, are the dives in the characteristic "passes." These are natural corridors through which the ocean water enters and leaves the atolls. The principal danger here are the currents that play in the external mouth, right where marine life flourishes. Nearly all the passes in the Maldives have the same characteristics: the entrance step is 114–131 feet high and the widths vary. One of the most famous is that of Felidu. Special mention must be made of Bushi Island where beautiful alcyonarias are found, and nurse sharks and eagle rays are also quite common. Only experts dive at these points as the currents are sometimes dangerous and they are distant from the coral reefs. Near the island of Abuhera lies a famous wreck, 459 feet long and practically impossible to photograph because the water is very cloudy. This is an impressive military transport ship. Distinctive also is the island of Fua Mulaki, where coral walls descend to the deepest of abysses. Here, it seems impossible to remain attached to the corals; the most expert divers allow themselves to float with the current, enjoying a truly thrilling spectacle.

A triton. Note its closed operculum, a "safety gate" for defense. Top: nudibranch eggs.

A nudibranch typical of warm seas; these are found in various colors.

It is impossible to lose yourself among the atolls of the Maldives. Even by night, in the absence of landmarks, the stars guide expert fishermen.

Of the Maldives' neneteen atolls, Suvadiva is one of the least polluted and most magical environments in the Indian Ocean. Its 240 islands are partially inhabited by fishermen and are marked east and west by vertiginous falls to frightening depths of up to 6,942 feet. The hunting of turtles and fishing is totally banned on the coral reef. Suvadiva is far from easy to reach as it can take up to sixteen hours to cross to it on the open sea through the equatorial canal. Perhaps this is why it is considered a pearl among underwater paradises.

Unpolluted paradises still exist in the Maldives. The temperature of the water varies between 80.6° and 84.2 °F and visibility is changed by the monsoons. The most expert scuba divers exploit the sea currents here; once they have ascended to a depth of 33 feet they allow themselves to be carried by the current entering the atoll. As they perform their decompression, the divers also explore long stretches of reef, that is until the current stops and green turtles up to 5 feet long start to emerge from the depths of the atoll.

# The Antilles

The Antilles has witnessed an explosion of diving centers. Most are American (Padi or Naui) but Cmas also has recently appeared. Particularly interesting are dives on the coral reef or along walls teeming with life. For the more experienced divers, there are guided dives on wrecks, some of which have become highly popular, for example, that of the Rhone, in the Virgin Islands, made famous by the film *Abyss*. Well marked are the diving points in the Netherlands Antilles, for example, at Bonaire. However, one of the most popular destinations is certainly Cuba, with its characteristic numbered buoys that correspond to different varieties of fish. Speaking of fish, Grand Bahamas is famous for its dives with dolphins and sharks. Everywhere, especially not far-off the coral reefs, you may see fauna and flora consisting of soft corals, gorgonians, and sponges in various colors, shapes, and sizes. The reefs offer a chance to meet countless varieties of colored fish such as barracudas, rays, moray eels, and the characteristic conches, Caribbean mollusks with a distinctive large shell, lobsters, and numerous sea turtles.

Left: a sponge formation.
Bottom Left: a *Pomacantus* or angelfish.

Opposite page: a distinctive soft, red and yellow coral.

The temperature of the waters varies between 78.8 and 84.2 °F for the whole year. The visibility is good between 66 and 164 feet of depth. In this sea it is advisable to use a wetsuit of 0.1 inches and sometimes also a subwetsuit.

# Sardinia

Sardinia is like the Caribbean islands of Europe. There are many top locations for scuba diving enthusiasts in the Mediterranean—Turkey, Medas, or even Malta as well as the Côte d'Azur—but enthusiasts hold a special place in their hearts for Sardinia. Despite its characteristic winds and cold sea even in the warmest months, a must-see are the red corals of Sardinia with fascinating dives offered on the Maddalena archipelago, also known as the "Mediterranean Polynesia" for its white sand and distinctive seabed with clear water. The most reputable spots for diving include Spargi, Spargiotto, Santo Stefano, Santa Maria, Caprera, Razzoli, and Budelli, famous for its pink sands. A succession of bays and inlets frames one of the most delightful underwater (practically uncontaminated) paradises that offers diverse vegetation such as Mediterranean maquis and seabeds of posidonia. Also of great interest are the shoals—particularly those of Washington and Punta Zanotto—perfect because they do not pose great difficulties or require expert skills to explore. Villasimius, in the province of Cagliari, offers its own special underwater paradise where courses are offered throughout the year at several levels. For years, underwater enthusiasts and professionals have met up at the Fiore di Maggio International Scuba Center, which offers numerous dives in the Geomarine park near Capo Carbonara.

Opposite page: a dolphin, an intelligent mammal that can be encountered quite frequently off Costa Paradiso.

With its spectacular corals and a typically Mediterranean seabed, Sardinia offers a special selection of dives.

Above: a hermit crab seeks refuge in sea anemones. Center Right: a spirographis.

Bottom Right: a mantis prawn. These are all typical inhabitants of the waters of Sardinia.

# Dives

**CARIBBEAN**

**CUBA**
All the waters around Cuba provide equally interesting dives and feature several species of brightly colored sponges—purple, red and blue—of indescribable dimensions. A great attraction are the cave visits, where the amusing silver-colored fish are not in the least bit intimidated by a human presence, and live inside and outside a vertical cavity along a very steep wall. There are many wrecks and settings for truly unique photographs and underwater videos.

**GRAND CAYMAN**
The beauty of these places and the increasing number of divers that visit the island's waters have resulted in the passing of a number of laws to protect this terrestrial paradise. Everything that surrounds Grand Cayman is stupendous, from the large gulf to the north coast. Two examples: the Rhapsody shoal that descends from 82 feet through the famous Wall to a vertiginous fall of 2624 – 2952 feet, an enchanting place with walls covered with sponges in myriad colors and fantastic dimensions and shapes. One encounter not to be missed is with the rays of Stingray City: a seabed just 13 feet deep over white sand where you will be surrounded by rays in just a few minutes.

**INDIAN OCEAN**

**RÉUNION**
An island in the center of the Ocean with a seabed of volcanic rock rich in corals and madrepores. Descending deeper you can observe the caves that have become the dens of huge barracudas and groupers weighing more than 44 pounds. There are numerous rock oases including the Roche Merveilleuse, rocks covered with golden gorgonians and, on the bottom, a shipwreck at more than 164 feet.

**ZABARGAD**
Zabargad is surrounded by a coral reef rich in various life forms. There are a few wrecks and a chance to make close encounters with the odd gray or hammerhead shark. Between the coast and the island lies. White Rock, which is the first of a number of coral reefs that make up the great St. John reef.

**PACIFIC OCEAN**

**FIJI**
Fiji is actually comprised of more than 300 islands, large and small, all gathered around the larger ones: Viti Levu and Vanua Levu. This archipelago has a common denominator: crystal clear water and billions of colors. On the island of Beqa, dives are not difficult because of the shallow depths, but beware of the strong currents in these waters. On the island of Taveuni you will find a unique wall: the Great White Wall, covered with white alcyonarias that give the impression you are swimming close to a huge underwater mountain covered with snow. The island of Matagi offers an extraordinary dive: the Golden Dream, an endless wall where everything, animal and vegetable, is a gilded yellow color.

**TONGA**
The location that first sees the dawn of the new day. In the Kingdom of Tonga, formerly Polynesia, everything is huge, from the sculptures fashioned by the wind to the human beings and the gigantic caves where the light creates spectacular effects. The locals free-dive to incredible depths. On the island of Vava'u is the cave of fans, a veritable forest of gorgonians, a unique underwater spectacle.

**NEW CALEDONIA**
This is an archipelago consisting of one large main island and a number of small islets that give rise to a series of lagoons and natural gulfs of extraordinary beauty. The most characteristic dives include that of the island of Pni, rich in underwater canyons and coral reefs, at the edge of which you may encounter large sharks. At the northern tip of the main island is Malabou with almost totally unexplored waters that are always crystal clear and rich in huge gorgonians plus sponges galore.

**GALAPAGOS**
Geologically, these are young lands and, together with Hawaii and the Canaries, represent one of the most important volcanic regions in the world. Crossed by sea currents of varying types, they feature a widely varied food content that supports exceptional underwater life. In the Galapagos, one of the most typical underwater encounters is with sea lions, clumsy animals out of the water but able swimmers in the island's waters. This delightful environment offers many possible dives: the Corona del Diablo, around a submerged crater; Champion, a small islet with clear water where you can photograph or film sea lions at play; Roca Redonda, a large rock where on the bottom you can spot the white finned sharks; and lastly, Darwin and Wolf, the two northernmost islands, which can be reached only after several days' sailing. The underwater spectacle is incredible: dozens of hammerhead sharks, barracudas, and eagle rays. If you are lucky you may even meet a killer whale.

| | |
|---|---|
| **RED SEA** | **SUDAN**<br>Diving in Sudanese waters is an experience that will remain in the soul of every diver: colors, living organisms, and fearsome but fascinating encounters. Jacques Cousteau came to the Shaab Rumi reef to study the behavior of whales, an encounter nearly guaranteed here. An "easy" dive can be made on Wingate Reef to visit the wreck of the Umbria, an Italian ship that was sunk by its own captain to prevent it from falling into British hands. A hole in the ship gives access to the hold, still full of old bottles and three old Fiat cars. |
| **MEDITERRANEAN** | **CORSICA**<br>The zone between Galeria and Capo Rosso is certainly one of the richest and most fascinating. The waters in the gulfs of Girolata and Porto are an example of the best the Mediterranean has to offer. One plus is that to encounter gorgonians, sponges, and other beautiful animal species it is not necessary to reach prohibitive depths. Around Bonifacio is the famous "grouper shoal," off the island of Lavezzi, where in addition to the spectacular marine environment on the seabed you may quickly be surrounded by five or six huge groupers. Another interesting point is that of the Calvi airplane wreck: a Flying Fortress, a B-17, landed on the sea and sank 330 feet from the bastions of the citadel of Calvi. Thanks to the crystal clear water you can even spot the outline of the wreck when snorkeling in the zone.<br><br>**CORFU**<br>This is the second largest island in the Ionian archipelago and has a truly fascinating underwater environment. Points of interest include Liapiades Reef, a shoal with walls that reach 197 feet; Colona Reef, close to the port of Paleokastrista, with a lovely cave full of prawns and large mantis. Not far away are the waters of the Colovri rock, where according to mythology lies the petrified ship of Ulysses. Of interest are the rocks of Lagudia where you can even free-dive to the wreck of an ancient ship that transported amphoras and vases. |
| **ITALY** | **ARGENTARIO**<br>Geologically the Argentario was an island that with the passing centuries and geological changes became a series of tongues of sand, turning it into a lagoon. There are many dives of interest: the island with a seabed 98 feet deep where you can come across the odd oyster; the Grotta Azzurra, in Cala de Santi, only 49 feet deep and therefore an excellent descent point even for novices and at night. Another characteristic point is the Argentarola rock, one of the most interesting dives on the Argentario.<br><br>**ISLAND OF TAVOLARA**<br>Sardinia offers hundreds of fascinating dives and the island of Tavolara is one of these. There are several shoals: Papa, Fico, Punta Arresto. One that must be mentioned is the islet of Reulino where on summer nights you are sure to encounter the Alicia mirabilis, a sea anemone with the sharpest sting in the Mediterranean, but also the most beautiful and sought after.<br><br>**FAVIGNANA**<br>An enchanting island, wild and rough, but uniquely poetic. One of the most attractive points is the Palumbo rock with the wreck of a cargo ship lying on one side at a depth of approximately 59 feet. This is an extremely tranquil and easily planned dive, even at night. The cave is approximately 98 feet long and leads to a natural lake. It is not unusual to meet octopi along it.<br><br>**LAKE CORNINO**<br>Italy is not just all about its surrounding seas, but also features many diverse lakes. In the north, particularly in the karst zone, many mysterious lakes conceal unique beauty and experiences. In Friuli there is Lake Cornino, with a surface area of approximately 10,166 square yards and a maximum depth of 26 feet. For dives here you must of course remember the rules for diving in freshwater and have suitable equipment for low temperature water. |

# Terminology

*continued from p. 104*

- **OPERCOLUM**
Bony gill cover on teleosteans.

- **P.A.D.I.**
Professional Association of Diving Instructors.

- **R.S.T.C.**
Recreational Scuba Training Center. This is the European body that seeks to impose uniform diver training and preparation standards that are recognized all over the world.

- **RECOVERY**
A course that trains a diver how to act in an emergency or dangerous situation, specific recovery techniques and prevention are studied.

- **REFITTING**
Together with tank removal, this is one of the basic movements in scuba diving technique training.

- **REGULATOR**
A device fed with oxygen that permits underwater breathing.

- **ROLL**
Typical movement required to pass from the surface to underwater.

- **S.S.I.**
Scuba School International.

- **SCUBA**
Self-Contained Underwater Breathing Apparatus, used on the most common basic course for diving at various levels.

- **SEARCH AND RECOVERY**
A professional branch of underwater activity specifically devoted to the search and retrieval of persons and things.

- **SHOAL**
A special conformation of the seabed that makes navigation difficult for divers. These are generally very interesting search and study areas for divers specialized in this sort of dive.

- **SNORKEL**
Tube used as an underwater breathing aid.

- **SNORKELING**
An initial approach to underwater activities, requiring only a mask, fins, a mouthpiece, and a serious support to practice.

- **STABILIZERS**
These are extensions of the foot pocket on fins.

- **TRITON**
A caudate amphibian with a distinctive flat tail.

- **VARIABLE BALLAST**
Descent with a weight maximum 66 pounds to the depth established, and an ascent with arms along a diving cable.

- **WEIGHT BELT**
A number of lead weights inserted in a special belt.

- **WETSUIT**
The diving garments that offer protection against both cold temperatures and possible accidents.

- **WRECK**
A sunken ship; in archaeological circles this indicates the carcass of ships run aground, found on the seabed.

**EDITOR:** Cristina Sperandeo

**TRASLATION:** Studio Queens, Milan

**Cover:** Opto Design

**PHOTOS:** Guido Ferri, Silvio Nestri, Maurillo Zucchiato
(94 left, 95, 98, 99, 114 right, 118 left, 119, 122, 123), Mimmo Drago (Mares Archives), Gianni
Risso (Mares Archives / Genoni's photography), Sector Archives.

Special thanks to Guido Ferri for his collaboration and technical advice,
to Silvio Nestri for his patience and confidence.
Grateful acknowledgment to Gianluca Genoni and Umberto Pelizzari
(Recordman), to Provincial Thecnical Center F.I.A.S. (Italian Association Underwater Activities) of
Milan, to Sardinia Agency Tourist Industries, to Mares,
to Sardinia Great Events, to Sector and to Technisub.

**GRAPHIC DESIGNER: CON**FUSIONE s.r.l.

**PRODUCTION:** G&G Computer Graphic s.n.c.

First Published in the United States of America in 2000
by UNIVERSE PUBLISHING
A Division of Rizzoli International Publication, Inc.
300 Park Avenue South
New York, NY 10010

2000 2001 2002 2003 2004 2005/ 10 9 8 7 6 5 4 3 2 1

Printed in Italy

ISBN 0-7893-0510-0